I0016401

Dan Gookin's
Guide to
Curl Programming

Dan Gookin's Guide to Curl Programming
Written by Dan Gookin

Published by Quantum Particle Bottling Co.,
Coeur d'Alene, ID, 83814
USA

Copyright ©2019 by Quantum Particle Bottling Co., Inc. All Rights Reserved.

Cover image by Dan Gookin and copyright ©2019 by Quantum Particle Bottling Co., Inc. All Rights Reserved.

For additional information on this or other publications from Dan Gookin and Quantum Particle Bottling Co., please visit http://www.wambooli.com/

Edition 1.0
October 2019

Table of Contents

TABLE OF CONTENTS 3

INTRODUCTION 9

ASSUMPTIONS 9
THE LIBCURL LIBRARY 10
CONVENTIONS 10
00-01_curlsample.c 11
CONTACTING THE AUTHOR 12

1. THE AMAZING CURL 13

USING CURL 13
Default curl 13
Curl command line 14
Configuration file 15
Usernames and passwords 17
FETCHING THINGS 18
Curl a web page 18
FTP 19
Other protocols 20
SENDING THINGS 20
FTP 21
HTTP POST 21
GETTING LIBCURL C CODE 23

2. THE LIBCURL LIBRARY 25

OBTAINING THE LIBRARY 25
Download the archive 25
The APT package manager 26
Homebrew on the Macintosh 26
CONFIGURING LIBCURL FOR THE CODE::BLOCKS IDE 27
A libcurl code::blocks project 27
Add the library 27
Locate the header files 28
TESTING INSTALLATION 29
The test program 29
02-01_curltest.c 29

Command line compilation *30*

Build in Code::Blocks *31*

Build in Xcode *31*

The verbose test program *32*

02-02_curlversion1.c *32*

Even more details test program *33*

02-03-curlversion2.c *33*

REVIEWING THE API *34*

3. YOUR BASIC WEB PAGE GRAB **35**

UNDERSTANDING THE LIBCURL PROCESS 35

Initialize the easy curl interface *35*

Set options *36*

Perform the curl operation *37*

Clean up the operation *37*

FETCHING A WEB PAGE 37

Basic web page fetch *38*

03-01_fetch1.c *38*

Basic fetch with error-checking *39*

03-02_fetch2.c *39*

More options *40*

FORWARDING THE REQUEST 42

Failure to forward *42*

03-03_follow1.c *42*

Follow the forwarder *43*

03-04_follow2.c *43*

REPORTING ERRORS 44

Set an error buffer *45*

03-05_curlerror1.c *46*

Even better error reporting *47*

03-06_curlerror2.c *47*

No error checking at all *48*

4. ADVANCED WEB PAGE GRAB **49**

SAVING A WEB PAGE TO A FILE 49

Open or create the output file *49*

Assign the options *50*

Close the file *51*

Sample code *51*

04-01_save2file.c (Lines 1 to 22) *51*

04-01_save2file.c (Lines 24 to 35) *52*

   04-01_save2file.c (Lines 37 to 55) *52*

SAVING BINARY DATA 53

   04-02_savedata.c *54*

STORING WEB DATA IN MEMORY 55

   The memory buffer structure *56*

   The callback function *56*

   Options to set *59*

   Sample code *60*

   04-03_savememory.c (Lines 1 to 10) *60*

   04-03_savememory.c (Lines 12 to 40) *60*

   04-03_savememory.c (Lines 42 to 47) *61*

   04-03_savememory.c (Lines 59 to 70) *61*

   04-03_savememory.c (Lines 72 to 90) *62*

5. CURL FTP 63

USING ANONYMOUS FTP TO GET A FILE 63

   Anonymous FTP setup *63*

   Sample code *64*

   05-01_anonftp.c (Lines 1 to 23) *64*

   05-01_anonftp.c (Lines 25 to 37) *65*

   05-01_anonftp.c (Lines 39 to 56) *65*

DEALING WITH PASSWORDS 66

   Username and password in the URL *66*

   The username and password option *67*

   Security concerns *68*

UPLOADING WITH FTP 68

   Upload a memory chunk *68*

   Sample code *69*

   05-02_ftpmemory.c (Lines 1 to 10) *69*

   05-02_ftpmemory.c (Lines 12 to 46) *70*

   05-02_ftpmemory.c (Lines 48 to 60) *71*

   05-02_ftpmemory.c (Lines 63 to 81) *71*

   05-02_ftpmemory.c (Lines 83 to 99) *72*

   Upload a file directly *73*

   05-03_ftpfile1.c (Lines 1 to 22) *74*

   05-03_ftpfile1.c (Lines 24 to 47) *75*

   05-03_ftpfile1.c (Lines 49 to 69) *75*

   05-03_ftpfile1.c (Lines 71 to 89) *76*

   Upload a file stored in memory *77*

   05-04_ftpfile2.c (Lines 1 to 11) *77*

   05-04_ftpfile2.c (Lines 13 to 39) *77*

05-04_ftpfile2.c (Lines 41 to 72) 78
05-04_ftpfile2.c (Lines 74 to 100) 79
05-04_ftpfile2.c (Lines 102 to 121) 80
05-04_ftpfile2.c (Lines 123 to 138) 81

6. MIME FORM DATA 83

FILLING IN THE BLANKS 83
Gather the details 84
Create the mime form..85
Sample code..87
06-01_mimeform.c (Lines 1 to 15)...87
06-01_mimeform.c (Lines 1 to 15)...88
06-01_mimeform.c (Lines 1 to 15)...88
Element options 90
UPLOADING A FILE AS MIME DATA..91
The upload form 91
Easy curl form data options 92
Sample code..93
06-02_formupload.c (Lines 1 to 19)...94
06-02_formupload.c (Lines 21 to 37)...94
06-02_formupload.c (Lines 39 and 40) 95
06-02_formupload.c (Lines 42 to 47)...95
06-02_formupload.c (Lines 49 to 54)...95
06-02_formupload.c (Lines 56 to 73)...96

7. FANCY CURL TRICKS...97

GOING VERBOSE...97
07-01_verbose.c 97
PROCESSING MULTIPLE FILES 98
EATING COOKIES 99
Cookie recipe 99
Website cookies 100
Libcurl cookies..101
07-02_cookie.c..101
GENERATING EMAIL 102
Various SMTP pieces..103
Sample code...107
07-03_mailsend.c (Lines 1 to 18) 107
07-03_mailsend.c (Lines 20 to 47) 108
07-03_mailsend.c (Lines 49 to 64) 109
07-03_mailsend.c (Lines 66 to 82) 109

07-03_mailsend.c (Lines 84 to 95) *110*

INDEX..**111**

ALSO BY DAN GOOKIN...**115**

Introduction

The *curl* utility is a command line tool that allows you to both send and retrieve files to and from the Internet. Its engine is libcurl, the C language library that empowers your programs to do the same amazing feats.

This book describes how to use the free libcurl library to access websites, use FTP to upload and download files, submit online forms, and more. The processes and functions are explained in a logical manner, along with plenty of easy-to-understand code examples to help you. Along the way, you have fun and are entertained as much as possible in a technology book.

Assumptions

This book assumes you know how to code in C; it's not a beginner book. Being able to code and create C programs, either at the command prompt or with an IDE, is vital.

Beyond knowing C, it helps to know a bit about your computer's operating system, where files are stored and how software can be downloaded and installed from the Internet.

I strongly recommend you have a knowledge of the terminal window in Unix or Windows. If you're using Linux, Unix, or Mac OS X, using the bash shell in a terminal window is perfect. Windows 10 users also have access to the bash shell, as described in Chapter 1.

Being a C coder, I assume you know how to use a compiler, either in an Integrated Development Environment (IDE) or at the command prompt.

This book covers configuring and using an IDE for writing C code incorporating the libcurl library. Examples are offered for the Code::Blocks IDE in Windows and Xcode on the Mac. To my knowledge, Microsoft Visual Studio doesn't allow third party libraries such as libcurl to be integrated into its projects.

Details for coding C at the command prompt in a terminal window are offered as well.

The Libcurl Library

The libcurl library is available free, as described in Chapter 2. Installation instructions are covered there, along with details on configuration for the various IDEs and command line compiling and linking.

Libcurl offers two methods for coding *curl* programs: easy and multi. These terms have nothing to do with the complexity of the code; easy isn't easier than multi so don't feel a stigma because you're coding something in easy curl.

This book uses the easy curl method of coding *curl* programs in C. The multi method allows for multiple *curl* operations through a single call to the multi interface. This technique isn't covered in this book, though it may be covered in a future edition.

Conventions

To consistently express programming lingo in the text, this book uses the following conventions:

C language keywords, library keywords, and function names appear in italic text, such as *printf()* and *char*.

Variable names, defined constants, and filenames appear in monospaced text, colored blue (if color is available): x and curl.h.

Functions are presented in a manner similar to the *man* page format:

```
CURL *curl_easy_init(void);
```

Variable types, such as the CURL pointer returned from the *curl_easy_init()* function above, are explained in the text, as are any arguments the function requires.

Sample code excerpts appear as follows:

```
struct MemoryStruct {
```

```
    char *memory;
    size_t size;
};
```

The text following the except explains the details.

Program code appears with the source filename first, followed by the code. The source filename uses chapter number, sequence number, followed by a unique name:

00-01_curlsample.c

```
1   #include <stdio.h>
2   #include <curl/curl.h>
3
4   int main()
5   {
6       CURL *curl;
7       char url[] =
8           "https://c-for-dummies.com/curl_test.txt";
9
10      curl = curl_easy_init();
11      curl_easy_setopt(curl, CURLOPT_URL, url);
12      curl_easy_perform(curl);
13      curl_easy_cleanup(curl);
14
15      return(0);
16  }
```

The line numbers to the left of the bar are for reference only; do not type them into your code.

I try to keep the demonstration programs in this book short and to the point. Some longer code examples are broken up into smaller chunks where I can provide comments for each section.

Comments in the code are limited and brief, mostly to keep the code short.

Because many libcurl function names are long, along with the defined constants, many statements in the sample code are split between two or more lines. This split avoids ugly wrapping that would otherwise take place in this narrow-column book.

Source code, sample files, and other resources are available on the companion website:

```
https://c-for-dummies.com/curl
```

Files are available individually or can be downloaded as an archive. I've also added "wide" versions of the source code files that don't split statements between multiple lines and include more comments for your reference.

Contacting the Author

Here is my email address:

`dgookin@wambooli.com`

I cannot promise to answer all email, though I don't mind saying "Hi" or addressing a programming puzzle directly tied to this book. I cannot troubleshoot your code for you, and I don't offer technical support on computer or compiler issues. Thanks for understanding.

My C language support website is:

`https://c-for-dummies.com/`

It features weekly C language lessons as well as monthly exercise challenges. You can also find online training at LinkedIn Learning, which is available for a subscription, though many of my courses have free previews:

`https://www.linkedin.com/learning`

Thank you for taking the time to read this introduction! So few people do. Losers. But you're different and show a tenacity that makes you the perfect libcurl programmer. Enjoy!

Dan Gookin,
October 2019

1. The Amazing Curl

Curl, or more accurately, cURL was born in the early days of the Internet. It's a two-part project that consists of a library, libcurl, as well as a command line utility, *curl*. Its purpose is to put or fetch information to or from the Internet by using a variety of protocols.

The name cURL stands for Client URL. The initialism URL stands for the Uniform Resource Locator. It's a web resource such as HTTP for a web page, FTP for file transfer, and so on.

Curl was developed by Daniel Stenberg and its home page is curl.haxx.se. (The *se* domain is for Sweden.)

Using *Curl*

Curl is a command line utility, thriving in the traditional text mode realm of using a computer. The command line today is found in a terminal window in Unix, Linux, or Mac OS X. Typically the terminal window runs the bash shell, which is what I use.

♦ *If curl isn't available, use the system's package manager to install it. The package name is* curl.

In Windows 10, you can install a Linux shell, from which you can run *curl*: Search the Microsoft Store for Linux and install your favorite distro. My choice is Ubuntu Linux.

If you have trouble installing a Linux shell in Windows 10, refer to this web page for assistance:

```
https://docs.microsoft.com/en-us/windows/wsl/install-win10
```

DEFAULT *CURL*

The simplest form of the *curl* command fetches a web page and coughs up its raw HTML text on the screen. The *curl* command is followed by the address of the page or document to fetch:

```
curl https://c-for-dummies.com/curl_test.txt
```

Upon success, the contents of the web page specified (a text file) are output to the terminal window:

```
Curl Read Test Successful

If you see this text in your terminal window as output,
libcurl has successfully read the online file!

Congratulations!
```

Try this command with any valid web page address to see how it works; the contents of the `curl_test.txt` document are used in Chapter 3 test the library's installation.

At its most basic form, however, the *curl* command is followed by a web page address to fetch and output the page's contents.

CURL COMMAND LINE

To provide for more control, options or switches are sandwiched between the *curl* command and the URL or address. These options set the type of transfer, specify a username and password, direct output to a file, and so on. The final option is the Internet resource requested – a URL or address.

Most options or switches have terse and verbose versions. For example, the switch to send output to a file can be `-o` (terse) or `--output` (verbose). Two dashes are used for verbose switches.

The full list of options and switches is found at the *curl* website:

```
https://curl.haxx.se/docs/manpage.html
```

This page echoes what you find in the *man* page, though as a web page it's easier to read and reference. The *curl man* page is found by typing **man curl** at the terminal window's command prompt.

The command prompt version of *curl* is quite versatile: Multiple URLs can be specified in a single command. Limited regular expressions can be used to capture them. For example:

```
curl http://{blog,store}.site.com
```

Above, *curl* fetches two web pages, one from `blog.site.com` and a second from `store.site.com`. Each word in braces (separated by commas) represents a different address for *curl* to access.

Sequences can be specified in square brackets:

```
curl http://site.com/pic[00-99].png
```

Above, *curl* retrieves files `pic00.png` through `pic00.png` from `site.com`. The effect is the same as issuing 100 separate *curl* commands or using *curl* on 100 different URLs. (Extra options must be specified with this command to ensure that the PNG images are saved to files and not output to the terminal as binary data.)

◆ *If the command interpreter doesn't recognize special symbols in an address, set the entire URL in double quotes.*

CONFIGURATION FILE

Curl commands can be quite complex, with multiple options and settings. To make things easier, you can split a long command across multiple lines. This trick is available to all commands issued in *bash* and similar shells, but I use it often with *curl*:

```
curl \
ftp://site.com/image1.jpg \
--user username:password \
--output image1.jpg
```

Each option, including the *curl* command itself, is followed by a space and backslash. These characters extend the command across several lines. The space ensures that options are separated.

The problem with this method is that the command becomes near impossible to edit should you goof up.

A better approach is to set the command and its options as separate lines in a configuration file. The following contents of such a file perform the same actions as the command line example above:

```
1  # FTP to fetch image
2  url = "ftp://site.com/image1.jpg"
3  user = username:password
4  output = "image1.jpg"
```

This file contains four lines:

Line 1 is a comment. The hash or pound sign prefix flags the following text on a line as a comment; such text is ignored by *curl*.

Line 2 sets the URL option, which includes the URL itself, FTP, and the name of the site to access including the filename to fetch, `image1.jpg`. You need not use double quotes to contain the URL unless it otherwise includes forbidden or potentially misinterpreted characters.

Line 3 sets the username and password for FTP access. This is the `--user` option set at the command prompt.

Line 4 sets the `--output` option, the name of the file to save locally.

This sample configuration file is saved as `ftp.site` (plain text). To direct the *curl* command at the prompt to use this configuration file, the `-K` (or `--config`) switch is specified:

```
curl -K ftp.site
```

After issuing the command, *curl* runs, accesses the FTP site, fetches and saves the named file per options set in the `ftp.site` configuration file.

As *curl* runs, a progress meter appears, as shown in Figure 1-1. This output can be suppressed by adding the `-s` or `--silent` switch to the list of commands.

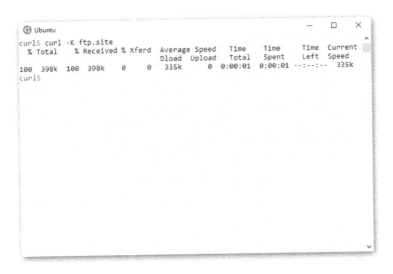

Figure 1-1: Curl's progress meter.

Another configuration file is available for global *curl* settings, ~/.curlrc. The ~ means the file is in your home directory and the dot as the first character of the filename means the file is hidden. You can use this file to set universal options for all *curl* commands; the contents of ~./curlrc are each time *curl* runs.

The commands put in the configuration file take the format:

option=setting

Where *option* is the command line switch (short or long version) and *setting* is a valid setting or string enclosed in double quotes. The equal sign can be replaced with any whitespace character. Escape characters can be used within double quotes. Each option must appear on a line by itself.

USERNAMES AND PASSWORDS

Passwords are specified in two ways when using *curl*: as part of a URL request or as a specific command line option.

As part of the URL, the format is:

```
curl url://user:pass@site.org/path
```

Where `url` is HTTP or FTP or whatever resource is requested where password access is required. The two slashes are followed by the username `user`, followed by a colon, then comes `pass` as the password, followed by an @ sign and the rest of the address.

A benefit to supplying the username and password as part of the address is that you can use URL encoding to specify otherwise un-typable, invalid, or conflicting characters. For example, if your password has a space in it, use %20:

```
curl url://dang:secret%20password@site.org/path
```

Above, `dang`'s password is `secret password`, which has a space (%20) in it.

Usernames and passwords can also be set as a command line option by using the -u or --user switch. The username and password are separated by a colon and they immediately follow the -u or --user switch.

```
curl -u user:pass url://site.org/path
```

This choice may seem more complex, but it can also be split across several lines and it's more consistent with the way libcurl sets up usernames and passwords when you code in C.

Fetching things

The *curl* utility's basic function is to snatch data from the Internet. It fetches web pages by default, but it can access other resources depending on the options set.

CURL A WEB PAGE

The *curl* command to pull down a web page is simple: *curl* followed by the web page address. For example:

```
curl site.org
```

The `site.org` website doesn't exist as this book goes to press. Assuming it did, the output you see might look like this:

```
<html>
 <head>
```

```
 <title>Site</title>
 </head>
 <body>
  <h1>Nothing Here!</h1>
 </body>
</html>
```

Curl downloads the page and outputs the text (raw HTML) to the screen. As shown in Chapter 3 this behavior is also the default for the libcurl library in your C code.

To save the web page text to a file, the -o switch (or --output) is used, and filename specified:

```
curl -o site.html site.org
```

The above command reads text from the site.org website, saving the results in the file site.html.

FTP

Curl automatically uses anonymous FTP to access file servers. For example:

```
curl ftp.site.org/d/file.txt -o file.txt
```

The above command uses the FTP protocol to access ftp.site.org. The login is anonymous. *Curl* automatically changes to directory d and gets file.txt. The -o switch saves the file to the same name locally, otherwise its contents would be sent to standard output.

◆ *It's important to use the -o (output) switch when downloading binary files. When you forget, curl reminds you.*

If an FTP login is required, use the -u or --user switch to specify your credentials:

```
--user username:password
```

The command can get quite long, so I often split it between several lines:

```
curl \
ftp.site.com \
--user user:pass
```

The backslash helps continue the command but remember to pad a space before the backslash or at the start of the next

19

line. Above, *curl* fetches a directory listing of the
`ftp.site.com` FTP site using the access ID `user` and
password `pass`.

To fetch a file, specify the filename in the URL:

```
curl \
ftp.site.com/dir/file.doc \
--user user:pass \
--output file.doc
```

The *curl* command, split between four lines, uses the FTP
protocol to get `file.doc` from the `dir` directory on `site.com`.
The username and password are specified, as well as the local
output file to which the data is saved.

FTP commands can get long! Remember you can stick
commands into a file if they get too cumbersome to type at
the prompt. The username and password can also be
included as part of the URL.

OTHER PROTOCOLS

Odds are good if you can fetch a file using some type of
protocol/URL, you can grab that file by using *curl*.

Options include FTPS, SFTP, SCP via SSH, and other fancy
acronyms, as well as various proxy servers.

One funky URL is DICT. I didn't know about this choice until
I began to research *curl* in depth. A DICT server is an online
dictionary, one of which (probably the only one) is `dict.org`:

```
curl dict://dict.org/d:obvious
```

The above *curl* command fetches the definition of the word
obvious from the `dict.org` dictionary server. The output is
plain text.

Sending things

The *curl* command can also upload files, using the same
protocols available for retrieving files – plus a few more. For
example, *curl* is a natural at FTP uploads, but it can also
upload using the HTTP protocol in the POST method. This
technique means you can use *curl* to submit form information

(fill-in-the-blanks) on a website. (Automation of form submissions is one reason why many pages feature a captcha that asks whether you're a robot.)

FTP

The -T switch (also --upload-file) is used at the command prompt to direct *curl* to upload a file to an FTP site. The switch is followed by the name of the local file to put to the site:

```
-T localfile.xlsx
```

As is often the case, a username and password must also be supplied to gain access to the site:

```
-u username:password
```

Or the username and password can be included in the URL, as described earlier in this book. Therefore, the command can grow long; refer to the earlier section "Configuration file" for details on including complex options in a text file that *curl* can read.

HTTP POST

Uploading via the HTTP protocol is done by posting text to a website. You've probably performed this task many times through filling in a web page form. The form is processed and sent to a web page, either as part of the URL (the GET method) or hidden (the POST method).

With *curl*, you can send information to a web page just as if it were filled in on a web page form. The text must be encoded as a single string, specified by using the -d or --data switch.

As an example, suppose a web page asks for the tidbits of information shown in Figure 1-2. The field names for this form are name, ssn, and pwd.

Vital Web Info

Name: [   ]

Social Security Number: [   ]

Password: [   ]

Figure 1-2: A typical web page form.

To submit the form, you must know the target page, the one that processes the data. Using the -d switch, you send a string with the completed fields formatted and concatenated, which can look like this:

```
"name=Dan%20Gookin&ssn=26&pwd=pass"
```

The entire string is enclosed in double quotes.

Each field is filled by setting the field name, an equal sign, then the field value using URL encoding. See the %20 in the name field? That's the space character.

Ampersands separate each field.

♦ *If the form uses a specialized* submit *button, it must be specified as* well.

The entire command can be rather lengthy. When using *curl* at the prompt, I split it between several lines like this:

```
curl \
http://site.com/receiver.php \
-d "name=Dan%20Gookin&ssn=26&pwd=pass"
```

The above command (spread across three lines) accesses web page receiver.php on site.com and sends the string specified via HTTP POST. If done correctly, the page processes the information and does whatever magic it's supposed to do.

When the web form specifies a file to be uploaded, use the -F switch to specify the file:

```
-F upload_file=@resume.docx
```

The filename is prefixed with an @ sign.

You can also specify the file's contents or MIME type:

```
-F "upload=@mugshot.png;type=image/png"
```

These examples show only the -F switch, but you must still include the receiving webpage in the command, along with whatever other options are required for command line *curl*.

Getting Libcurl C code

Curl can do far more than what I've documented in this Chapter. Its capabilities are extensive, which are fully documented on the `curl.haxx.se` website. Yes, it's easy to get lost in the site's abundance of detail.

One trick worthy of note is how command line *curl* helps you code programs in C. In fact, it's almost like cheating.

The `--libcurl` switch, followed by an output filename, generates C code that uses the libcurl library to perform the same action as command line *curl*.

For example:

```
curl https://c-for-dummies.com/curl_test.txt \
--libcurl test.c
```

The above command fetches a text document from `https://c-for-dummies.com`. The page's contents are sent to standard output. Also, a file is generated, `test.c`. In the file is C code that performs the same action.

The sample code generated in `test.c` (from the above command) is 46 lines long. It contains all the options set by the *curl* command, some of which aren't completely necessary when coding in C. The code even includes options not set but which you can investigate to see what they do. (The code is complex and, unfortunately, is too wide to show in this narrow-page book.)

You can compile the C code generated to generate a program that performs the same action as the *curl* command.

In fact, if you can create a *curl* command at the prompt, and it works the way you like, you can add the `--libcurl` switch to get the code you need. It's generated instantly and accurately. At that point, you can use the code or modify and hone it to match your needs.

2. The Libcurl Library

The libcurl library is the engine behind the *curl* utility. Both were developed together. This relationship means that anything you can do with *curl* at the command prompt you can do with your C programs by using the libcurl library.

Obtaining the library

You can seize the libcurl library from the `curl.haxx.se` website, downloading its archive. For Linux users, use your distro's package manager to install the library for command-line programming. On the Macintosh, use the Homebrew utility. These options are each covered later in this section.

After obtaining and installing the library, see the section "Testing installation" for the next step.

DOWNLOAD THE ARCHIVE

The Download page on the Curl website lists source code archives as well as packages for specific operating systems. Visit the page at:

`https://curl.haxx.se/download.html`

The items under Source Archives represent the source code files, which you can expand and build on your machine.

Packages are organized by operating system or Linux distribution. For Linux and the Mac, I recommend using a package manager for more effective installation.

The download archives and package names include a version number. Try to obtain the latest, stable release, which is highlighted in yellow on the download page. The stable release may not be the latest version.

♦ *The Windows version is either 32 bit or 64 bit, depending on the Windows installation. It is compatible with Code::Blocks as shown later in the section, "Configuring libcurl for the Code::Blocks IDE."*

THE APT PACKAGE MANAGER

In Linux, use the operating system's package manager to obtain and install the libcurl library. This process can take place in the GUI or at the command prompt in a terminal window.

For example, many Linux distros use the Advanced Package Tool or *apt* to obtain and install new software. This tool is also available in many of the Windows 10 Linux shells.

To install libcurl, type this command:

```
sudo apt-get install libcurl4-gnutls-dev
```

The *sudo* command activates the Super User account, which lets you install system-wide software. You must type the Super User password to proceed. (This password may be your own account password, depending on how Linux is configured.)

`apt-get install` directs *apt* to install the named package, `libcurl4-gnutls-dev` in this case.

After installation, you're ready to run a test program to confirm that everything ran smoothly.

HOMEBREW ON THE MACINTOSH

Homebrew is the "missing package manager" for the Macintosh. It's available from `brew.sh`. Open a terminal window on the Mac and follow the directions on that page to install Homebrew.

Once installed, use the following command in a terminal window to install the libcurl library for development on the Mac:

```
brew install libcurl
```

The libcurl libraries and header files are installed in the Unix side of the Macintosh. You can use the terminal window to build the demonstration programs offered in this book.

Sample programs in this book can also be run in Xcode, as described in the later section, "Build in Xcode."

Configuring libcurl for the Code::Blocks IDE

If you use Code::Blocks in Windows, you can add the libcurl library and its functions to your C code quite easily. This process avoids using the command prompt for programming, though creating the programs becomes more involved. The key is to specify the libcurl library and the location of the libcurl header files for your Code::Blocks project.

The procedures documented here may also apply to using Code::Blocks on the Macintosh, though my experience with CB on the Mac isn't as pleasant as it is in Windows.

Libcurl may also work with other IDEs, though I'm aware that Microsoft Visual Studio doesn't allow the inclusion of third-party libraries in its projects.

A LIBCURL CODE::BLOCKS PROJECT

To start a new C program that uses the libcurl library in Code::Blocks, obey these steps:

1. Choose File, New, Project.

It must be a new project; you cannot link in the libcurl library for an individual source code file.

2. Select Console Application and click Go.
3. Choose the C language and click Next.
4. Give the project a title and optionally select a folder, click Next.
5. Select the Release configuration and click Finish.

The project file is created and a dummy `main.c` source code file presented. The source code file is found in the Workspace window in the project's branch: Open *Sources* to locate it.

ADD THE LIBRARY

To ensure that the libcurl library is linked into your project, follow these steps:

1. Choose Project, Build Options.

The Project Build Options dialog box appears. It lists two sets of tabs.

2. Choose the Linker Settings tab from the top row of tabs.
3. In the Link Libraries area, click the Add button.

You must add the libcurl library to the project.

4. Click the Browse button (the open folder) to browse to the location where the libcurl library was installed.

These steps assume you've downloaded the Windows version of the library. Further, that you know in which folder the library files are installed. You must browse to that location for Code::Blocks to include the library.

Within the installation folder, look for the `lib64` (or `lib32`) folder, which contains the library files.

5. Select the `libcurl.a` library.

The file may have a longer name that includes a timestamp. Even so, it should start with `libcurl` and have the `.a` (dot-A) filename extension.

6. Click the Open button.
7. I recommend clicking No to retain an absolute path to the library file.
8. Click the OK button to add the library to your project.

Keep the Project Build Options dialog box open to add the header file location, as described in the next section.

LOCATE THE HEADER FILES

Continuing from the preceding section, your next steps inform the project where to look for the libcurl header files. This folder is `include/curl` and it's found where you installed the libcurl library:

9. In the Project Build Options dialog box, click the Search Directories tab.
10. Ensure that the Compiler tab is chosen from the second set of tabs. Further ensure that the Policy option is Append Target options to Project Options.
11. Click the Add button.

12. In the Add Directory dialog box, click the Browse (open folder) icon.

13. Browse to the folder where you installed the libcurl library, include **folder.**

14. Choose the `include` folder.

You don't want to choose the `curl` folder, as libcurl code assumes header files take the format:

```
#include <curl/curl.h>
```

15. Click No to keep the absolute path.

16. Click the OK button to add the search path.

17. Click OK to close the Project Build Options dialog box.

You're done configuring Code::Blocks to link in the libcurl library and locate the header files. You can now test the installation.

Testing installation

Whenever I install a new C language library, I write a quick test program. The code outputs the library's version number, which is usually held as a defined constant declared inside one of the header files. By including the constant, the compiler confirms that header file installation was successful.

To further test installation, I also link in the library. Even though the sample code lacks any library functions, by linking the library I'm assured that the linker can locate it.

Upon success, I know that my test program worked, and that the library was properly installed.

THE TEST PROGRAM

The source code in this section is used to test the libcurl library's installation. This code is available, like all source code files mentioned in this book, on the companion website: `c-for-dummies.com/curl`

02-01_curltest.c

```
1  #include <stdio.h>
2  #include <curl/curl.h>
3
```

```
4   int main()
5   {
6       printf("libcurl version %s\n", LIBCURL_VERSION);
7
8       return(0);
9   }
```

The libcurl header file `curl/curl.h` is included at Line 2. The compiler expects to find the header files in a `curl` directory located where header files are stored. Traditionally this location is `/usr/include` in Unix, though it might also be `/usr/local/include`. The location might also be relative to your IDE or wherever the package manager chooses to install the library.

The *printf()* statement outputs the `LIBCURL_VERSION` string constant.

Here's a sample run:

```
libcurl version 7.58.0
```

The version number you see may be different from what's shown in this text.

COMMAND LINE COMPILATION

At the bash command prompt in a terminal window, type this command to compile and link the `02-01_curltest.c` source code:

```
clang -Wall -lcurl 02-01_curltest.c
```

Clang is the name of the compiler. You can also use *gcc* or *cc*, though *clang* offers intelligent warnings and suggestions. (The *clang* LLVM compiler can be installed by using your operating system's package manager; search for *clang*.)

I prefer to use the `-Wall` switch to activate all warnings.

The `-lcurl` switch directs the linker (dash little L) to look for and link in the `curl` library.

The source code filename comes last.

Press Enter to compile and link the code. Upon success, the program `a.out` is created in the current directory.

If you encounter any errors, confirm the location of the header file and libraries.

♦ *On some systems, specifically when you see a parade of linker errors, you may need to specify the* `-lcurl` *switch last.*

To run the program, type this command:

```
./a.out
```

The `./` prefix directs the command interpreter to look in the current directory for the named file, `a.out`. The output shows you the current libcurl library version.

BUILD IN CODE::BLOCKS

Start a new project in Code::Blocks, as described earlier in this book. Ensure that you've linked in the libcurl library and set the search location for the header files.

Type the source code shown earlier into the `main.c` file or add the `02-01_curltest.c` source downloaded from the companion website. Build and run to test.

♦ *Remember to close the output window after testing a program in Code::Blocks. If you leave the output windows open, the IDE may start to act funky.*

BUILD IN XCODE

If you run Xcode on the Macintosh, and have installed the libcurl library, you can use it as your IDE to build the sample programs presented in this book.

For example, to compile the sample code presented earlier in this section, heed these steps in the Xcode IDE:

1. Choose File, New, Project.
2. For the template, choose MacOS.
3. Select the Command Line Tool as the Application.
4. Click the Next button.
5. Name the project.

This test program project could be named `02-01_curltest` or just Curl Test.

6. **Ensure that C is chosen as the language.**
7. **Click the Next button.**
8. **Choose a folder in which to save the project.**

A project window appears.

9. **From the left side of the window, open the project's folder and double-click on the** main.c **source code file.**
The source code appears in an editor at the center of the project window.

10. **Paste or type the code from the sample source code file into the** main.c **file, replacing the existing code skeleton.**
11. **Save the project: chose File, Save.**
12. **Click the Run button at the top left of the project window, (It looks like a Play icon, a triangle.)**

The program's output appears in the lower right corner of the project window.

♦ *You can also use the terminal window to code at the command prompt, as described earlier in this Chapter.*

THE VERBOSE TEST PROGRAM

If you truly want to confirm that the library is linked in and working, you can use the *curl_version()* function to return a detailed string describing the curl version – and more.

The *curl_version()* function has this format:

```
char *curl_version(void);
```

The function takes no argument and returns a string (*char* pointer) representing the version number.

The following source code is based on 02-01_curltest1.c, but replaces the LIBCURL_VERSION defined constant with the *curl_version()* function:

02-02_curlversion1.c

```
1  #include <stdio.h>
2  #include <curl/curl.h>
3
4  int main()
5  {
```

```
6        printf("libcurl version %s\n", curl_version());
7
8        return(0);
9    }
```

Here's the output:

```
libcurl version libcurl/7.58.0 GnuTLS/3.5.18 zlib/1.2.11
libidn2/2.0.4 libpsl/0.19.1 (+libidn2/2.0.4)
nghttp2/1.30.0 librtmp/2.3
```

You can spy the version number in there: 7.58.0. Also included is other libraries and their version numbers. Details, details.

EVEN MORE DETAILS TEST PROGRAM

To pluck out those details you want to know about the libcurl library, use the *curl_version_info()* function:

```
curl_version_info_data *curl_version_info(CURLversion age);
```

Its argument is a *CURLversion* variable, typically the constant CURLVERSION_NOW, for the current version. The function returns a *curl_version_info_data* structure pointer, which contains way too many members to list here. The full document is available on the Curl website:

```
https://curl.haxx.se/libcurl/c/curl_version_info.html
```

The following code plucks out only the current libcurl version. It uses the *version* member of the *curl_version_info_data* structure:

02-03-curlversion2.c

```
1    #include <stdio.h>
2    #include <curl/curl.h>
3
4    int main()
5    {
6        curl_version_info_data *data;
7
8        data = curl_version_info(CURLVERSION_NOW);
9        printf("libcurl version %s\n", data->version);
10
11       return(0);
12   }
```

The program's output is identical to the earlier sample code:

```
libcurl version 7.58.0
```

Reviewing the API

The libcurl API (Application Programming Interface) is quite extensive. As a happy bonus, it's also well-documented, complete with plenty of examples and sample code. For a full libcurl library reference, refer to the online documentation at:

```
https://curl.haxx.se/docs/
```

3. Your Basic Web Page Grab

Just like *curl* at the command prompt, the most basic function of a libcurl C program is to fetch a webpage. The page's text is sent to standard output.

As with any C program, a bit of overhead is required when coding a basic libcurl fetch: special variables are created, options must be set, and steps taken in a specific order.

Understanding the libcurl process

The libcurl library's easy curl interface sends or retrieves information to or from the Internet in a four-step process.

1. Create a *CURL* handle, like a *FILE* handle
2. Set options for the *CURL* handle
3. Perform the easy curl operation
4. Clean up

The key to the entire procedure is Step 2 where options are set and the operation is customized. This step works like setting options for *curl* at the command prompt, though each one is set by using a specific function as a statement in your code.

INITIALIZE THE EASY CURL INTERFACE

The easy curl interface works like opening a file in C. Instead of the *FILE* handle, the libcurl library uses a *CURL* handle, a pointer variable that keeps track of the fetch or send process:

```
CURL *curl
```

Above, the *CURL* handle variable `curl` is created. As with the *FILE* variable, it's a pointer.

A *CURL* handle is returned from the *curl_easy_init()* function. This function has no arguments and it requires inclusion of the `curl/curl.h` header file:

```
CURL *curl_easy_init(void);
```

I recommend you test the value of the pointer returned with the NULL constant to ensure that the operation was successful. If the value returned is NULL, easy curl has failed to initialize.

Upon success, the *CURL* handle variable is used throughout the rest of the code, serving like a *FILE* handle in the various functions that control the fetching or sending operation.

SET OPTIONS

Setting options is the most involved part of the process; the libcurl library has dozens of different features and settings, many of which echo command line options for *curl*.

The option-setting function is *curl_easy_setopt()*:

```
CURLcode curl_easy_setopt(
  CURL *handle,
  CURLoption option,
  parameter
);
```

The three arguments are:

- A *CURL* file handle
- A *CURLoption* constant representing the option to set
- A parameter related to the option

For example, to set the URL – the address of a web page to fetch – the constant CURLOPT_URL is used. The parameter (third argument) is the URL string:

```
curl_easy_setopt(curl, CURLOPT_URL, "http://site.org");
```

Above, curl is the *CURL* handle returned from the *curl_easy_init()* function. The CURLOPT_URL constant informs the *curl_easy_setopt()* function to expect a URL as the third argument, which is the string http://site.org in this example.

In a typical libcurl program, you find multiple *curl_easy_setopt()* statements, especially for complex operations. These options control libcurl's behavior.

◆ *A common value for the third argument is* 1L *(one* long)*, which activates an option. The argument* 0L *(zero* long) *deactivates an option.*

36

PERFORM THE CURL OPERATION

After the mess of options are set, a single statement thrusts libcurl into action, venturing out to the Internet to perform whatever marvels you desire.

The function that sets libcurl into action is *curl_easy_perform()*:

```
CURLcode curl_easy_perform(CURL * easy_handle );
```

The function's sole argument is the *CURL* handle returned from the *curl_easy_init()* function. The value returned is a *CURLcode* variable, which can be tested for errors. Here's an example:

```
r = curl_easy_perform(curl);
```

Above, `curl` is a *CURL* handle. The value returned, `r`, can be compared with the constant CURLE_OK to confirm the operation's success, though libcurl also outputs its own error messages.

The *CURLcode* value returned from *curl_easy_perform()* can also be used as the argument of the *curl_easy_strerror()* function to offer more descriptive text about the boo-boo. Refer the section "Even better error reporting" later in this Chapter for details.

CLEAN UP THE OPERATION

The final step in the easy curl process is similar to using the *fclose()* function to close a file. To do so, use the *curl_easy_cleanup()* function with the *CURL* handle as its argument:

```
void curl_easy_cleanup(CURL * handle );
```

The function's single argument is the *CURL* handle returned earlier from the *curl_easy_init()* function. This function returns no value.

Fetching a web page

As with the *curl* command, the most basic operation for a libcurl program is to fetch a web page's text and send its contents to standard output. The process of performing this task requires a minimum of libcurl functions – though you can pack in more if you want your code to be thorough.

BASIC WEB PAGE FETCH

To output a web page's contents – raw HTML or plain text – requires four libcurl functions in four statements that echo the four steps outlined at the start of this Chapter. Here's the code:

03-01_fetch1.c

```
1   #include <stdio.h>
2   #include <curl/curl.h>
3
4   int main()
5   {
6       CURL *curl;
7       char url[] =
8           "https://c-for-dummies.com/curl_test.txt";
9
10      /* initialize easy curl */
11      curl = curl_easy_init();
12
13      /* set options */
14      curl_easy_setopt(curl, CURLOPT_URL, url);
15
16      /* curl */
17      curl_easy_perform(curl);
18
19      /* cleanup */
20      curl_easy_cleanup(curl);
21
22      return(0);
23  }
```

Line 6 declares the *CURL* variable `curl`. I apologize for the lack of creativity.

The `url` variable at Line 7 is split between two lines, thanks to its length and this book's narrow margins.

Line 11 initializes the easy curl interface (Step 1).

Line 14 uses *curl_easy_setopt()* to specify the URL to fetch, which is a special text file I've made available on my *C For Dummies* website (Step 2).

Line 17 performs the *curl* operation (Step 3).

Line 20 cleans up easy curl (Step 4).

Compile and link this code to see what it does. When run, you may notice a delay. This pause is the program venturing out to the Internet to fetch the URL.

If the program errs, you see an error message output by libcurl. Most often it's a connection error. If so, try again.

Upon success, you see output similar to the following:

```
Curl Read Test Successful

If you see this text in your terminal window as output,
libcurl has successfully read the online file!

Congratulations!
```

Congratulations, indeed.

BASIC FETCH WITH ERROR-CHECKING

As an active C programmer and instructor, I continually try to improve my code, specifically to make it run safe. The sample code shown earlier in 03-01_fetch1.c is absent error-checking that would make the program more secure. The following improvement corrects this omission:

03-02_fetch2.c

```
1    #include <stdio.h>
2    #include <stdlib.h>
3    #include <curl/curl.h>
4
5    int main()
6    {
7        CURL *curl;
8        CURLcode r;
9        char url[] =
10           "https://c-for-dummies.com/curl_test.txt";
11
12       /* initialize easy curl */
13       curl = curl_easy_init();
14       if( curl == NULL)
15       {
16           fprintf(stderr,"curl init fail\n");
17           exit(1);
18       }
19
20       /* set options */
21       curl_easy_setopt(curl, CURLOPT_URL, url);
```

```
22
23    /* curl */
24    r = curl_easy_perform(curl);
25    if( r!=CURLE_OK )
26    {
27        fprintf(stderr,"curl fail");
28        exit(1);
29    }
30
31    /* cleanup */
32    curl_easy_cleanup(curl);
33
34    return(0);
35 }
```

At Line 14, the `curl` pointer variable returned from the
curl_easy_init() function is tested against the `NULL` constant. If
true, easy curl didn't initialize properly, an error message is
output, and the program quits.

The value returned from *curl_easy_perform()* at Line 24 is
retained in *CURLcode* variable `r`. This value is tested at Line
25 against the `CURLE_OK` constant. If false, the *curl* operation
failed. The value in `r` can further be tested to output a specific
error message, described later in this chapter.

MORE OPTIONS

This same *curl* operation at the command prompt to fetch the
page at `https://c-for-dummies.com/curl_test.txt`,
coupled with the `--libcurl` option, generates quite different
sample code from the earlier examples. The code sets
multiple options and makes suggestions to set even more.

For example, the code sets the following:

```
curl_easy_setopt(curl, CURLOPT_BUFFERSIZE, 102400L);
```

The `CURLOPT_BUFFERSIZE` option sets the preferred buffer size
(above) to about a megabyte. This is a request, so no
guarantee is made that such a large buffer would be used.
The default writing buffer size, `CURL_MAX_WRITE_SIZE`, is 16K;
the default reading buffer size, `CURL_MAX_READ_SIZE`, is 512K.
The minimum size is 1024 bytes.

```
curl_easy_setopt(curl, CURLOPT_NOPROGRESS, 1L);
```

The CURLOPT_NOPROGRESS constant disables the output progress bar when the third argument is 1L (one *long*). Specifying 0L (zero *long*) as the third argument activates the progress bar. Refer to Figure 1-1 to see what the progress bar looks like.

```
curl_easy_setopt(curl,CURLOPT_USERAGENT,"curl/7.58.0");
```

The CURLOPT_USERAGENT constant supplies a null-terminated string in the HTTP request header. Above, the string informs the server that the request is made from *curl* version 7.58.0.

The user agent request helps a server recognize who or what is making the call – the client. The format includes the client name first, followed by a slash and a version number. This string is how some web pages can identify which computer or web browser you're using. It's not a requirement to supply this information with your libcurl requests.

```
curl_easy_setopt(curl, CURLOPT_MAXREDIRS, 50L);
```

The CURLOPT_MAXREDIRS constant informs libcurl of how many times to follow a webpage forwarding, or redirect, request. This option is used with CURLOPT_FOLLOWLOCATION to heed forwarding request built into certain webpages. See the next section.

```
curl_easy_setopt(curl, CURLOPT_HTTP_VERSION,
(long)CURL_HTTP_VERSION_2TLS);
```

The CURLOPT_HTTP_VERSION constant supplies information in the request header about the HTTP version to use. The third argument is a *long* integer value, a constant setting the HTTP version. In the sample call above, the version is HTTP 2 over TLS (HTTPS), with fallbacks to earlier versions. HTTP version constants are documented online at:

```
https://curl.haxx.se/libcurl/c/CURLOPT_HTTP_VERSION.html
```

```
curl_easy_setopt(curl, CURLOPT_TCP_KEEPALIVE, 1L);
```

The CURLOPT_TCP_KEEPALIVE constant, with the third argument set to 1L (one *long* for "active" or "on"), directs libcurl to send TCP keepalive packets to the host to maintain the connection.

More information on these options, as well as all the *curl_easy_setopt()* constants, can be found on the libcurl documentation page:

```
https://curl.haxx.se/libcurl/c/curl_easy_setopt.html
```

Forwarding the request

Many websites automatically forward a URL request to a new page or updated service. For example, when the site domain has changed security or when a mobile device requests a version of the page formatted for that device, in these cases a forwarding request automatically redirects the visitor to the updated address.

In libcurl, you direct your code to obey a forwarding request by using the *curl_easy_setopt()* function with the CURLOPT_FOLLOWLOCATION constant as the second argument and setting 1L (one *long*) as the third option:

```
curl_easy_setopt(curl,CURLOPT_FOLLOWLOCATION,1L);
```

Setting this option ensures that whatever redirects the website stipulates are handled automatically.

FAILURE TO FORWARD

If you update the earlier code, 03-02_fetch2.c to change the URL from an HTTPS request (secure) to HTTP, the curl operation fails.

03-03_follow1.c

```
9 | char url[] = "http://c-for-dummies.com/curl_test.txt";
```

The only change made to the code is at Line 9, shown above. (Refer to the companion website for the full source code listing, which is otherwise identical to 03-02_fetch2.c.)

Upon building and running this code, the following output is generated:

```
<!DOCTYPE HTML PUBLIC "-//IETF//DTD HTML 2.0//EN">
<html><head>
<title>301 Moved Permanently</title>
</head><body>
<h1>Moved Permanently</h1>
```

```
<p>The document has moved <a href="https://c-for-
dummies.com/curl_test.txt">here</a>.</p>
</body></html>
```

This HTML text informs the user that the document (page) has moved and generates a link to the new site. This kind of embarrassment can be avoided by setting the CURLOPT_FORWARDLOCATION option before making the call to *curl_easy_perform()*.

FOLLOW THE FORWARDER

To direct libcurl to obey the forwarding directions, you add another *curl_easy_setopt()* function with the CURLOPT_FORWARDLOCATION constant as the second argument. The third argument is 1L. This addition can be made to the code in the preceding example, 03-03_follow1.c, by adding the following statement after Line 20:

```
curl_easy_setopt(curl,CURLOPT_FOLLOWLOCATION,1L);
```

Here is the complete, updated code listing:

03-04_follow2.c

```
1    #include <stdio.h>
2    #include <stdlib.h>
3    #include <curl/curl.h>
4
5    int main()
6    {
7        CURL *curl;
8        CURLcode r;
9        char url[] =
10           "http://c-for-dummies.com/curl_test.txt";
11
12       /* initialize easy curl */
13       curl = curl_easy_init();
14       if( curl == NULL)
15       {
16           fprintf(stderr,"curl init fail\n");
17           exit(1);
18       }
19
20       /* set options */
21       curl_easy_setopt(curl, CURLOPT_URL, url);
22       curl_easy_setopt(curl,CURLOPT_FOLLOWLOCATION,1L);
23
24       /* curl */
25       r = curl_easy_perform(curl);
26       if( r!=CURLE_OK )
```

```
27      {
28          fprintf(stderr,"Curl fail");
29          exit(1);
30      }
31
32      /* cleanup */
33      curl_easy_cleanup(curl);
34
35      return(0);
36  }
```

When the CURLOPT_FOLLOWLOCATION option is set, shown at Line 22, the web page request is forwarded. The output is what's expected:

```
Curl Read Test Successful

If you see this text in your terminal window as output,
libcurl has successfully read the online file!

Congratulations!
```

Forwarding requests are also affected by the option CURLOPT_MAXREDIRS. The third argument (*long*) in the *curl_easy_setopt()* function directs libcurl to follow that number of redirects maximum, no more. The value can be set to 0L (zero *long*), which disables redirection or -1L (negative one *long*) which sets an infinite number of redirects.

Reporting errors

When the *curl_easy_perform()* function fails, it returns a value other than CURLE_OK. You can test this value in your code and output a generic error message. For example:

```
r = curl_easy_perform();
if( r != CURLE_OK )
{
    fprintf(stderr,"Some kinda error!\n");
    exit(1);
}
```

Variable r is of the *CURLcode* variable type. When it doesn't match the CURLE_OK constant, it holds an error number, which can be interpreted further.

SET AN ERROR BUFFER

The libcurl library provides options to output more sophisticated error messages. For example, you can create a *char* buffer to store a message supplied by the library itself. Use the *easy_curl_setopt()* function to identify the buffer and it's filled with an error message should the easy curl operation go south.

The buffer is declared as a *char* array with its size set to the constant CURL_ERROR_SIZE. For example:

```
char errbuff[CURL_ERROR_SIZE];
```

The *char* buffer (string) effbuff is used later in the code should an error occur.

To inform libcurl about the error buffer, use the *curl_easy_setopt()* function with the CURLOPT_ERRORBUFFER constant set as the second argument and the buffer name as the third:

```
curl_easy_setopt(curl,CURLOPT_ERRORBUFFER,errbuff);
```

The buffer's contents come into play when the result of the *curl_easy_perform()* operation isn't equal to CURLE_OK. Your code handles such a situation like this:

```
if( r!=CURLE_OK )
{
    fprintf(stderr,"Can't curl %s\n",url);
    fprintf(stderr,"Error: %s\n",errbuff);
    exit(1);
}
```

In this code snippet, the text stored in errbuff is output when the value of variable r isn't equal to CURLE_OK. For example:

```
Can't curl odd://site.com
Error: Protocol "odd" not supported or disabled in
libcurl
```

The following code shows a full example of how to set the error buffer option to output an error message should easy curl fail:

45

03-05_curlerror1.c

```
1   #include <stdio.h>
2   #include <stdlib.h>
3   #include <curl/curl.h>
4
5   int main()
6   {
7       CURL *curl;
8       CURLcode r;
9       char url[] = "odd://site.com";
10      char errbuff[CURL_ERROR_SIZE];
11
12      /* Initialize easy curl */
13      curl = curl_easy_init();
14      if( curl == NULL)
15      {
16          fprintf(stderr,"Unable to init curl\n");
17          exit(1);
18      }
19
20      /* set options */
21      curl_easy_setopt(curl,CURLOPT_URL,url);
22      curl_easy_setopt(curl,CURLOPT_ERRORBUFFER,errbuff);
23
24      /* curl the resource */
25      r = curl_easy_perform(curl);
26      if( r!=CURLE_OK )
27      {
28          fprintf(stderr,"Can't curl %s\n",url);
29          fprintf(stderr,"Error: %s\n",errbuff);
30          exit(1);
31      }
32
33      /* cleanup */
34      curl_easy_cleanup(curl);
35
36      return(0);
37  }
```

Line 10 creates the `errbuff[]` array with its size set to `CURL_ERROR_SIZE`.

At Line 22, the `CURLOPT_ERRORBUFFER` option is set. The function's third argument is the `errbuff[]` array where the error message, if any, is stored.

Should the *curl_easy_perform()* function err, the `errbuff[]` array's contents are output at Line 29.

The program fails in this example because the fetched URL, `odd://site.com`, uses a weird protocol I made up. The error message output is the same as shown before the source code listing. In fact, if you attempt to *curl* odd://site.com at the command prompt, you see a similar error:

```
curl: (1) Protocol "odd" not supported or disabled in
libcurl
```

Such output is useful for debugging purposes and provides more informative for the user than a generic message.

EVEN BETTER ERROR REPORTING

The advantage of storing an error message in a buffer is that the code can examine it, parse the text, compare the string to a known value, and potentially deal with the problem. A better way to output errors is to use the *curl_easy_strerror()* function:

```
const char *curl_easy_strerror(CURLcode errornum);
```

The function's argument is the _CURLcode_ error code value, such as that returned from the *curl_easy_perform()* function. Its return value is a null terminated string containing a relevant error message. This message isn't necessarily identical to the one set by using the *curl_easy_setopt()* function with the CURLOPT_ERRORBUFFER constant, covered in the preceding section.

The following code demonstrates using the *curl_easy_strerror()* function. It appears at Line 28, nestled in an *fprintf()* function that I split across three lines.

03-06_curlerror2.c

```
1   #include <stdio.h>
2   #include <stdlib.h>
3   #include <curl/curl.h>
4
5   int main()
6   {
7       CURL *curl;
8       CURLcode res;
9       char url[] = "odd://site.com";
10
11      /* Initialize easy curl */
12      curl = curl_easy_init();
13      if( curl == NULL)
14      {
```

```
15          fprintf(stderr,"Unable to init\n");
16          exit(1);
17      }
18
19      /* set options */
20      curl_easy_setopt(curl, CURLOPT_URL, url);
21
22      /* curl the resource */
23      res = curl_easy_perform(curl);
24      if( res!=CURLE_OK )
25      {
26          fprintf(stderr,"Can't curl %s\n",url);
27          fprintf(stderr,"Error: %s\n",
28                  curl_easy_strerror(res)
29              );
30          exit(1);
31      }
32
33      /* cleanup */
34      curl_easy_cleanup(curl);
35
36      return(0);
37  }
```

Here's output from a sample run:

```
Can't curl odd://site.com
Error: Unsupported protocol
```

NO ERROR CHECKING AT ALL

Libcurl outputs some error messages itself, such as
connection errors or when a site is unreachable. If you omit
error checking of the value returned from the
curl_easy_perform() function in either of the two preceding
sample programs, no output is generated upon the error.
Therefore, I recommend you use error checking in your code
to help keep the user – and yourself – informed.

Sample code with no error checking, `03-07_curlerror3.c`, is
available on the companion website.

4. Advanced Web Page Grab

The default behavior for both *curl* at the command prompt and code created by using the libcurl library is to send the fetched web page to standard output. This behavior can be altered by setting various options.

With *curl* at the command prompt, you can send output to a file by using the -o or --output switch. You can perform the same feat with libcurl – saving data as a file or even saving it to a buffer – providing you set options before making the easy curl call.

Saving a web page to a file

Redirecting libcurl's output to a file involves three steps:

1. Open or create a file to store the data
2. Set various easy curl options
3. Close the file after the operation is complete.

First, the code must open a file for output. Use standard C I/O functions to accomplish this task.

Second, options are set by using the *curl_easy_setopt()* function to direct the easy curl interface to send data received to the open file.

Finally, after the easy curl operation is complete, you must close the file as part of the clean-up process.

The following sections provide details for each step in the process.

OPEN OR CREATE THE OUTPUT FILE

It's up to you to open or create the output file; libcurl doesn't do it for you. This basic I/O duty can be accomplished by using the standard C library *fopen()* function:

```
fh = fopen("output.html","w");
```

The file named `output.html` is created for writing, "w", its handle saved in *FILE* pointer `fh`.

As always, test the file handle returned against the `NULL` constant to ensure the file opened (was created) properly:

```
if( fh==NULL )
{
    fprintf(stderr,"Some kinda error\n");
    exit(1);
}
```

Libcurl handles writing to the file. Your job is to open it set an easy curl option that specifies the open *FILE* handle variable, then close the file.

ASSIGN THE OPTIONS

With the file open, your next step is to direct libcurl to output incoming text to the file. Two options must be set: the write callback function and the file handle.

The write function

The write function, also referred to as the callback function, is the part of your code that handles data received from the Internet.

To set the write function, use the *curl_easy_setopt()* function with the `CURLOPT_WRITEFUNCTION` constant set as the second argument. The third argument specifies the name of the function that handles incoming data. For standard output to a file, set this argument to `NULL`. This choice directs libcurl to write to the open file handle – but that file handle must also be set as an option.

Specify the open file handle

To inform libcurl of the open file handle, to which data must be written, you must call the *curl_easy_setopt()* function with the constant `CURLOPT_WRITEDATA` as the second argument. The open file handle is the third argument:

```
curl_easy_setopt(curl, CURLOPT_WRITEDATA, fh);
```

Combined with setting the CURLOPT_WRITEFUNCTION option, data pulled from the web is written to the open file.

CLOSE THE FILE

The final step in the process is to close the open file. Use the *fclose()* (or similar companion statement), as you would to close an open file:

```
fclose(fh);
```

The *fclose()* statement can appear any time after the *curl_easy_perform()* function is called. I typically place it after the *curl_easy_cleanup()* function.

♦ *If the program must bail before clean-up, remember to close the open file before exiting.*

SAMPLE CODE

The following code puts together the pieces to write web page text to a file, output.txt. I've split the code into chunks for easy browsing.

04-01_save2file.c (Lines 1 to 22)

```
1   #include <stdio.h>
2   #include <stdlib.h>
3   #include <curl/curl.h>
4
5   int main()
6   {
7       CURL *curl;
8       CURLcode r;
9       char address[] =
10          "https://c-for-dummies.com/curl_test.txt";
11      char filename[] = "output.txt";
12      FILE *fh;
13
14      /* open fh file */
15      fh = fopen(filename,"w");
16      if( fh==NULL )
17      {
18          fprintf(stderr,"Can't create '%s'",
19              filename
20              );
21          exit(1);
22      }
```

Lines 9 and 10 specify the URL in variable `address`, split between two lines to avoid ugly wrapping in this text.

The file is opened at Line 15 and confirmed at Line 16.

04-01_save2file.c (Lines 24 to 35)

```
24      /* initialuze curl */
25      curl = curl_easy_init();
26
27      /* set options */
28      curl_easy_setopt(curl,
29          CURLOPT_URL,address);
30      curl_easy_setopt(curl,
31          CURLOPT_FOLLOWLOCATION, 1L);
32      curl_easy_setopt(curl,
33          CURLOPT_WRITEFUNCTION, NULL);
34      curl_easy_setopt(curl,
35          CURLOPT_WRITEDATA, fh);
```

Line 25 initializes the easy curl interface, then the following statements set options. I split the statements between two lines to avoid ugly wrapping.

The write callback function is set to NULL at Lines 32 and 33. Libcurl handles writing to the file directly.

Lines 34 and 35 specify the open file's handle, `fh`, which directs libcurl to send data received to the open file.

04-01_save2file.c (Lines 37 to 55)

```
37      /* read the address */
38      r = curl_easy_perform(curl);
39      if( r != CURLE_OK )
40      {
41          fprintf(stderr,"curl failed: %s\n",
42              curl_easy_strerror(r)
43              );
44          fclose(fh);
45          exit(1);
46      }
47
48      /* cleanup and close */
49      curl_easy_cleanup(curl);
50      fclose(fh);
51      /* let the user know what's going on */
52      printf("File '%s' written\n",filename);
53
54      return(0);
55  }
```

The file is fetched at Line 38 with the *curl_easy_perform()* function. Line 49 cleans up easy curl. Line 50 closes the open file.

The code specifically outputs a message at Line 52 to inform the user that the file is written. Otherwise, the code would have no output on success.

Here's output from a sample run:

```
File 'output.txt' written
```

The contents of output.txt reflect the web page specified. In this example, it's the demo text used throughout this book:

```
Curl Read Test Successful

If you see this text in your terminal window as output,
libcurl has successfully read the online file!

Congratulations!
```

If an error occurs, an appropriate error message is output.

Saving binary data

Not everything you can grab from the web is text. You can also use libcurl to fetch binary data, such as an image file, archive, or other non-text files.

The process for saving such data works the same as for fetching text. The only change required is the name of the file to download. Also, I recommend that you set the *fopen()* function's second argument to `"wb"` to write binary data.

The source code file 04-02_savedata.c demonstrates how to capture a binary download. It's is identical to 04-01_safe2file.c with the following differences:

```
 9      char address[] =
10          "https://curl.haxx.se/logo/curl-logo.svg";
```

The value of the address[] array is changed at Line 10 to reflect the web location of the curl logo file, curl-logo.svg.

```
11      char filename[] = "curl-logo.svg";
```

At Line 11, the output `filename` is set to the name of the curl logo file.

```
15 |     fh = fopen(filename,"wb");
```

And the "wb" argument is set at Line 15.

Here is the full source code listing, with the altered statements underlined:

04-02_savedata.c

```
1    #include <stdio.h>
2    #include <stdlib.h>
3    #include <curl/curl.h>
4
5    int main()
6    {
7        CURL *curl;
8        CURLcode r;
9        char address[] =
10           "https://curl.haxx.se/logo/curl-logo.svg";
11       char filename[] = "curl-logo.svg";
12       FILE *fh;
13
14       /* open fh file */
15       fh = fopen(filename,"wb");
16       if( fh==NULL )
17       {
18           fprintf(stderr,"Can't create '%s'",
19               filename
20               );
21           exit(1);
22       }
23
24       /* initialuze curl */
25       curl = curl_easy_init();
26
27       /* set options */
28       curl_easy_setopt(curl,
29           CURLOPT_URL,address);
30       curl_easy_setopt(curl,
31           CURLOPT_FOLLOWLOCATION, 1L);
32       curl_easy_setopt(curl,
33           CURLOPT_WRITEFUNCTION, NULL);
34       curl_easy_setopt(curl,
35           CURLOPT_WRITEDATA, fh);
36
37       /* read the address */
38       r = curl_easy_perform(curl);
39       if( r != CURLE_OK )
40       {
41           fprintf(stderr,"curl failed: %s\n",
42               curl_easy_strerror(r)
```

```
43              );
44          fclose(fh);
45          exit(1);
46      }
47
48      /* cleanup and close */
49      curl_easy_cleanup(curl);
50      fclose(fh);
51      /* let the user know what's going on */
52      printf("File '%s' written\n",filename);
53
54      return(0);
55  }
```

The address to curl is shown at Line 10, the Curl homepage on the Internet. The filename is specified as part of the URL, `curl-logo.svg`. This filename is also assigned to string `filename` at Line 11. The file is an SVG image.

Here's a sample run:

```
File 'curl-logo.svg' written
```

If you examine the directory in which the program runs, you'll find a new file added, `curl-logo.svg`. This image file can be viewed in a web browser or any compatible graphics program.

Storing web data in memory

Sending web data to a file isn't the only course of action. You can also save the downloaded information to a buffer, where it can be examined or modified.

As an example, say you're downloading JSON data and would prefer to store it in memory for easy manipulation. The process is similar to saving data to a file, but the dance is more intricate.

The key difference is that a memory buffer structure is created to hold the incoming data. Rather than setting the callback function to NULL, as was done for saving a file directly, an actual callback function must be written. This function manages the incoming data.

The following sections ruminate upon these details.

THE MEMORY BUFFER STRUCTURE

To handle a dynamic chunk of data, a resizable buffer is used. This buffer is referenced by using what I call the memory buffer structure, a structure defined by libcurl as:

```
struct MemoryStruct {
  char *memory;
  size_t size;
};
```

The structure can be given any name; *MemoryStruct* is used in libcurl documentation. The two members can also have unique names, but their data types are required: a *char* pointer to reference the buffer itself, and a *size_t* value reflecting the number of bytes (characters) in the buffer.

The *char* pointer must be allocated and initialized before information is read from the Internet. This step is handled by using the *malloc()* function to set aside a single byte of storage:

```
webdata.memory = malloc(1);
```

Above, the *MemoryStruct* structure variable `webdata` has its *memory* member assigned to reference a single byte of storage. This allocation must be tested against the `NULL` constant to ensure that memory was properly allocated.

The *size_t* member represents the number of bytes stored in the buffer. Its value must also be initialized, typically to zero (despite one byte being allocated to the memory buffer):

```
webdata.size = 0;
```

Once initialized, the structure is identified by setting an easy curl option, as described later.

THE CALLBACK FUNCTION

Don't sweat the callback function: It's fully documented in the libcurl API. In fact, most programmers copy-and-paste this code and call it good. You're better than that, of course.

The function can be called whatever you like, though the API documentation uses the function name *write_callback()*:

```
size_t write_callback(
  char *ptr,
  size_t size,
  size_t nmemb,
  void *userdata
);
```

The function's data type is static *size_t*; it returns the buffer's size upon success.

The function is also declared *static* so that it retains its values between calls. (The *static* keyword isn't shown in the function definition above.)

The callback function has four arguments:

char *ptr is the location of a chunk of data fetched from the Internet. This information is copied to the local buffer, referenced in the memory buffer structure.

size_t size represents a single item in the memory chunk, similar to the size argument in the *fread()* or *fwrite()* functions.

size_t nmemb This argument refers to the number of size items in the memory chunk. The size and nmemb items are multiplied together to get the memory chunk's actual size.

void *userdata is the address of the memory buffer structure (from the preceding section). This argument provides your code access to the data chunks read from the Internet.

Effectively, the callback function's goal is to transfer information from the ptr address used by libcurl to the userdata structure used by your code.

Two other variables are declared and used within the callback function:

size_t realsize represents the product of the size and nmemb arguments.

struct MemoryStruct mem is a pointer that holds the value of the userdata argument locally within the function. It's necessary to typecast the argument, which arrives as a *void* pointer. This variable references your code's memory buffer structure.

Here's a sample callback function:

```
static size_t write_mem(
    void *ptr,
    size_t size,
    size_t nmemb,
    void *userdata)
{
    size_t realsize;
    struct web_data *mem;

    realsize = size * nmemb;
    mem = (struct web_data *)userdata;

    mem->buffer = realloc(mem->buffer,
        mem->size + realsize + 1);
    if( mem->buffer==NULL )
    {
        fprintf(stderr,"Memory error\n");
        exit(1);
    }

    memcpy( &(mem->buffer[mem->size]),
        ptr,
        realsize);
    mem->size += realsize;
    mem->buffer[mem->size] = 0;

    return(realsize);
}
```

Many of the statements in this function are split between two lines to avoid ugly text wrapping.

Within the function, the following steps occur:

```
realsize = size * nmemb;
```

The number of bytes retrieved is stored in the `realsize` variable.

```
mem->buffer=realloc(mem->buffer,mem->size+realsize+1);
```

The memory buffer, `mem->buffer`, is reallocated to accommodate the freshly arrived chunk of data. The *realloc()* function resets the buffer's size to its current size, `mem->size`, plus the incoming data chunk, `realsize`, plus one. The resulting pointer is compared with `NULL` to ensure that the operation is successful.

58

```
memcpy( &(mem->buffer[mem->size]), ptr, realsize);
```

The *memcpy()* function copies `realsize` bytes from the `ptr` (first argument) buffer into the memory buffer structure. This function requires that you include the `string.h` header file in your code.

```
mem->size += realsize;
```

The *size* member of the memory buffer structure is updated to reflect the buffer's new size.

```
mem->buffer[mem->size] = 0;
```

Finally, the last byte of the memory buffer is set to zero.

OPTIONS TO SET

Once the memory buffer is declared and the callback function written, you must inform easy curl. This step requires two calls to the *curl_easy_setopt()* function, both of which are also used to write incoming data to a file.

The first option is `CURLOPT_WRITEFUNCTION`, which identifies the callback function by name:

```
curl_easy_setopt(curl,CURLOPT_WRITEFUNCTION,write_mem);
```

The function's first argument is the *CURL* handle. The second argument is the constant, `CURLOPT_WRITEFUNCTION`. The final argument is the name of the callback function, *write_mem*. (When saving data to an open file, the final argument is `NULL`.)

The second option to set uses the `CURLOPT_WRITEDATA` constant to identify the data chunk to manage within the callback function, the memory buffer structure:

```
curl_easy_setopt(curl,CURLOPT_WRITEDATA,(void *)&chunk);
```

The third option is the address of the *MemoryStruct* structure, `chunk` in this example, which is typecast as *void*.

After setting these and potentially other options, the *curl_easy_perform()* call is made and the rest of the action is automatic.

SAMPLE CODE

The following code grabs a text file at `c-for-dummies.com`
and saves it in memory. The chunk stored in memory is then
output.

This code uses shorter names than you find in the API
documentation, primarily to keep the text from wrapping in
this book. I've split the code into easily digestible chunks:

04-03_savememory.c (Lines 1 to 10)

```
1  #include <stdio.h>
2  #include <stdlib.h>
3  #include <string.h>
4  #include <curl/curl.h>
5
6  /* memory buffer structure */
7  struct web_data {
8      char *buffer;
9      size_t size;
10 };
```

The memory buffer structure is named `web_data` in this code.
It has two members, *buffer* and *size*. The structure is declared
externally to ensure that all functions can reference it.

04-03_savememory.c (Lines 12 to 40)

```
12  /* callback function */
13  static size_t write_mem(
14      void *ptr,
15      size_t size,
16      size_t nmemb,
17      void *userdata)
18  {
19      size_t realsize;
20      struct web_data *mem;
21
22      realsize = size * nmemb;
23      mem = (struct web_data *)userdata;
24
25      mem->buffer = realloc(mem->buffer,
26          mem->size + realsize + 1);
27      if( mem->buffer==NULL )
28      {
29          fprintf(stderr,"Memory error\n");
30          exit(1);
31      }
32
33      memcpy( &(mem->buffer[mem->size]),
34          ptr,
```

```
35          realsize);
36      mem->size += realsize;
37      mem->buffer[mem->size] = 0;
38
39      return(realsize);
40  }
```

The write callback function starts at Line 13. Its purpose is to transfer data read from the Internet into the user-supplied memory buffer, as described earlier.

04-03_savememory.c (Lines 42 to 47)

```
42  int main()
43  {
44      CURL *curl;
45      CURLcode r;
46      char address[] =
47          "https://c-for-dummies.com/curl_test.txt";
48      struct web_data page;
49
50      /* initialize storage structure */
51      page.buffer = malloc(1);
52      if( page.buffer==NULL )
53      {
54          fprintf(stderr,"Memory error\n");
55          exit(1);
56      }
57      page.size = 0;
```

The code sets the address of the page to download at Lines 46 and 47, split between two lines to avoid wrapping in this text.

At Line 51 the memory buffer structure's *buffer* member is allocated, and the pointer confirmed.

Line 57 sets the buffer's size to zero.

04-03_savememory.c (Lines 59 to 70)

```
59      /* initialuze curl */
60      curl = curl_easy_init();
61
62      /* set options */
63      curl_easy_setopt(curl,
64          CURLOPT_URL,address);
65      curl_easy_setopt(curl,
66          CURLOPT_FOLLOWLOCATION,1L);
67      curl_easy_setopt(curl,
68          CURLOPT_WRITEFUNCTION,write_mem);
69      curl_easy_setopt(curl,
70          CURLOPT_WRITEDATA,(void *)&page);
```

Line 60 initializes the easy curl interface. Options are set starting at Line 63.

The write callback function is specified at Lines 67 and 68. The memory buffer structure is set at Lines 69 and 70.

04-03_savememory.c (Lines 72 to 90)

```
72      /* read the address */
73      r = curl_easy_perform(curl);
74      if( r != CURLE_OK )
75      {
76          fprintf(stderr,
77              "curl read failed: %s\n",
78              curl_easy_strerror(r));
79          exit(1);
80      }
81
82      /* cleanup */
83      curl_easy_cleanup(curl);
84
85      /* output results */
86      printf("Read %ld bytes:\n", page.size);
87      printf("%s",page.buffer);
88
89      return(0);
90  }
```

Line 74 performs the file-reading action, processing the web page into memory for storage.

Line 83 cleans up easy curl.

Lines 86 and 87 outputs the number of bytes downloaded and stored and displays the memory buffer's contents.

Because the data fetched is small, this program probably calls the *write_mem()* function only once. If the data chunk were larger, the function would be called repeatedly, each time enlarging the storage buffer by the number of bytes fetched from the Internet. This is the entire purpose of the callback function: to accommodate for and store data read without knowing beforehand how much storage is required.

5. Curl FTP

FTP is the name of a program and a protocol for sending and receiving files over a network. It stands for File Transfer Protocol, which means saying "FTP protocol" is redundant.

The *ftp* client program uses the FTP protocol to send and receive files in an interactive manner. Connection is made to an FTP server, which handles the requests.

FTP is also a URL, which means *curl* is more than up to the task of sending and receiving files just like using the *ftp* program.

Curl can fetch FTP data quite easily, especially when anonymous FTP is used, which doesn't require authentication to access the server.

When FTP requires authentication, the interactive *ftp* program prompts for a username or password. For *curl*, the username and password can be specified as part of the URL or by using the -u or --user command line switch.

Libcurl handles these FTP processes adeptly. The key is to set the proper options. A read or write callback function is also required for some advanced operations.

Using anonymous FTP to get a file

When I need to use anonymous FTP, I skip using the *ftp* program and go straight to *curl*. The single command may be more complex than using *ftp*'s interactive interface, but it's solid and easy.

ANONYMOUS FTP SETUP

Coding a libcurl program to fetch a file anonymously from an FTP site is similar to saving a webpage to a file, though it requires five steps:

1. Specify the URL and filename.
2. Open a file for output.
3. Set the write callback options.

4. Let libcurl do the work.
5. Close the file.

The URL is specified by using the full address of the FTP site, including a pathname to the file you want to fetch. For example:

```
char ftp[] = "ftp://127.0.0.0/file.pdf";
```

The FTP site above is a placeholder; it would be replaced with a legitimate, anonymous FTP server.

Open the file for output, setting the "wb" (write binary) argument in the *fopen()* statement if the file retrieved is non-text.

For anonymous FTP, you don't need to code a callback function. Just as with saving a webpage to a file, you must set options by using the *curl_easy_setopt()* function with two constants:

Use the CURLOPT_WRITEFUNCTION constant with NULL as the third argument. This option directs libcurl to write its output directly to the open file.

Use the CURLOPT_WRITEDATA constant with the open file handle as the third argument.

Call *curl_easy_perform()* to fetch the file. Remember to use *fclose()* on the open file handle before the code exits. This includes using *fclose()* in case *curl_easy_perform()* fails.

SAMPLE CODE

The following code is very similar to what's required for fetching a web page and saving it to a file. The big difference is the address, which is an FTP site, shown at Line 12. The rest of the code is pretty much the same.

This code has been split into easily digestible chunks.

05-01_anonftp.c (Lines 1 to 23)

```
1   #include <stdio.h>
2   #include <stdlib.h>
3   #include <string.h>
4   #include <curl/curl.h>
```

```
 5
 6   int main()
 7   {
 8       char ftp[] = "ftp://127.0.0.0/file.pdf";
 9       CURL *curl;
10       CURLcode r;
11       FILE *fh;
12       char filename[] = "file.pdf";
13
14       /* open output file */
15       fh = fopen( filename, "wb");
16       if( fh==NULL)
17       {
18           fprintf(stderr,
19               "Can't create %s\n",
20               filename
21               );
22           exit(1);
23       }
```

The FTP URL specified at Line 8 is a placeholder, though a
filename, file.pdf, is appended. The filename is also defined
at Line 12.

The local file is opened for writing at Line 15.

05-01_anonftp.c (Lines 25 to 37)

```
25       /* initialize curl */
26       curl = curl_easy_init();
27
28       printf("FTP...");
29       /* set options for FPT fetch */
30       curl_easy_setopt(curl,
31           CURLOPT_URL, ftp);
32       curl_easy_setopt(curl,
33           CURLOPT_FOLLOWLOCATION, 1L);
34       curl_easy_setopt(curl,
35           CURLOPT_WRITEFUNCTION, NULL);
36       curl_easy_setopt(curl,
37           CURLOPT_WRITEDATA, fh);
```

The CURLOPT_WRITEFUNCTION and CURLOPT_WRITEDATA
options are set at Lines 34/35 and 36/37. As with saving a
web page to a file, the write function is set to NULL and the
write data option is set equal to the handle of the open file,
fh.

05-01_anonftp.c (Lines 39 to 56)

```
39       /* request-send upload */
40       r = curl_easy_perform(curl);
```

```
41    if( r!=CURLE_OK )
42    {
43        fprintf(stderr,"curl error: %s\n",
44            curl_easy_strerror(r));
45        fclose(fh);
46        exit(1);
47    }
48
49    /* cleanup */
50    curl_easy_cleanup(curl);
51    fclose(fh);
52    /* inform the user */
53    printf("File '%s' written\n",filename);
54
55    return(0);
56 }
```

The open file is closed at Line 51, though if the *curl_easy_perform()* function fails, it's closed within the *if* statements at Line 45.

At Line 53, a text message is output to confirm that the data has been written.

Here's a sample run, assuming a legitimate, anonymous FTP URL was supplied at Line 8:

```
FPP...File 'file.pdf' written
```

Dealing with passwords

You have two options for setting a username and password when the FTP request requires authentication.

First, you can specify the username and password as part of the URL.

Second, you can use the *curl_easy_setopt()* function to set the username and password.

The following sections provide the details.

USERNAME AND PASSWORD IN THE URL

This trick isn't specific to *curl* because you can embed any username and password in a URL. Here's the format:

```
protocol://username:password@domain.com/path/
```

The *protocol* is the URL, such as HTTP, FTP, and what-have-you. It's followed by the colon and two slashes.

Next come the *username* and *password*, separated by a colon. An @ sign trails the password.

The rest of the address is as expected: a *domain* name, a path, and potentially a specific file.

Here's a sample FTP address with a username and password as part of the URL:

```
ftp://user:pass@127.0.0.0/dir/file.pdf
```

The username is `user`, password is `pass`. The rest of the address is the domain, "home," or `127.0.0.0`, then the directory `dir` and the file `file.pdf`.

Any unusual characters in the username or password must be URL encoded. For example, a space would appear as %20, where 20 is the hexadecimal value of the space character (ASCII 32):

```
ftp://user%20name:pass@127.0.0.0/file.pdf
```

Above, the username is `user name`, with a space embedded.

Likewise, if an @ sign is in the username or password, it must URL encoded as %40.

THE USERNAME AND PASSWORD OPTION

The username and password can also be specified by using the *curl_easy_setopt()* function. This function requires three arguments:

- A *CURL* handle, returned from the *curl_easy_init()* function
- The defined constant CURLOPT_USERPWD
- A string representing the username and password, each separated by a colon

Here's a sample statement setting the username and password as an easy curl option:

```
curl_easy_init( curl, CURLOPT_USERPWD, "user:pass");
```

67

The *CURL* handle is named `curl`. The username is `user` and the password is `pass`.

It's important that the string specified as the third argument represent the exact username and password; URL encoding cannot be used. This limitation means that if either the username or password contains the colon character (`:`), you must set the username and password as part of the address string by using URL encoding for the colon (`%3A`) instead of setting this option in libcurl.

For sample code using the `CURLOPT_USERPWD` constant, refer to the later section, "Uploading with FTP."

SECURITY CONCERNS

I would advise against hard coding a username and password. Instead, consider putting such secure information in a separate file or somehow encrypting the details to keep your code secure.

After using the username and password, consider filling their buffer with null characters or otherwise zeroing out their storage area so that snooping programs can't pull such vital information from the program.

Uploading with FTP

For a libcurl FTP operation, especially one that requires a username and password, things can get busy quickly. As with saving a web page to a file, a memory buffer structure and callback function are required to upload a file. Depending on whether the file must be opened or its data already sits in memory, however, the level of complexity varies.

UPLOAD A MEMORY CHUNK

Say you have data in a chunk of memory – something that you loaded from one or more files, transferred in from another location, or created from scratch. To reference that buffer, use the memory buffer structure, the same one used in libcurl for storing a web page in memory:

```
struct MemoryStruct {
  char *memory;
  size_t size;
};
```

The structure's members describe the data for an easy curl action: The *memory* member holds the address of the buffer's base. The *size* member holds its size – including any null character at the end of a string.

The FTP address contains the site name, password options, and the directory where you want the buffer sated. This string ends with the filename, as in:

```
char address[] = "ftp://127.0.0.0/dir/file.bin";
```

The `address` variable identifies an ftp server at `127.0.0.0` and saves the memory chunk in the `dir` directory using the filename `file.bin`.

Options are set by using the *curl_easy_setopt()* function to identify the memory buffer structure as well as the read callback function.

The read callback function is what spoon-feeds the data from memory for uploading. As with the write callback function, it monitors the buffer to ensure that a proper-sized chunk of data is accessed.

SAMPLE CODE

The details for an FTP memory upload process are shown in the following sample code, which uses libcurl to FTP a string to a website. Be aware that the FTP address, username, and password are placeholders in this code.

The code is broken into chunks for easy reference and viewing.

05-02_ftpmemory.c (Lines 1 to 10)

```
1   #include <stdio.h>
2   #include <stdlib.h>
3   #include <string.h>
4   #include <curl/curl.h>
```

```
 5
 6    /* memory buffer structure */
 7    struct data_chunk {
 8        char *buf;
 9        size_t size;
10    };
```

At Line 7, the memory buffer structure *data_chunk* is declared externally as it's referenced in both the *read_callback()* and *main()* functions.

05-02_ftpmemory.c (Lines 12 to 46)

```
12    static size_t read_callback(
13        void *ptr,
14        size_t size,
15        size_t nmemb,
16        void *user_data)
17    {
18        struct data_chunk *upload;
19        size_t max;
20
21        /* initialize local pointer */
22        upload = (struct data_chunk *)user_data;
23        /* calculate number of bytes to write */
24        max = size*nmemb;
25
26        /* if nothing to write, return zero */
27        if(max<1)
28            return(0);
29
30        /* move the data chunk into buffer */
31        if(upload->size)
32        {
33            if(max > upload->size)
34                max = upload->size;
35            memcpy(ptr, upload->buf,max);
36            /* increase the pointer's base to
37                reference the next chunk */
38            upload->buf += max;
39            /* adjust the buffer size */
40            upload->size -= max;
41
42            return(max);
43        }
44
45        return(0);
46    }
```

The read callback function starts at Line 12. It uses a standard definition, similar to the callback function for downloading a file. The goal here, however, is to read *from* the buffer as opposed to building (expanding) the buffer: Data is transferred from the `user_data` argument to libcurl's storage, the `ptr` argument.

The key statement is the *memcpy()* function at Line 35. It copies data from the user's buffer to the `ptr` buffer used by libcurl for uploading.

05-02_ftpmemory.c (Lines 48 to 60)

```
48  int main()
49  {
50      char ftp_upload[] = "ftp://127.0.0.0/test.txt";
51      char user_pass[] = "username:password";
52      char text[] = "This text is uploaded\n";
53      CURL *curl;
54      CURLcode res;
55      struct data_chunk ftp;
56      int bufsize;
57
58      bufsize = strlen(text) + 1;
59      /* initialize the memory buffer */
60      ftp.buf = text;
61      ftp.size = bufsize;
```

In the *main()* function, the "upload buffer" is a string, `text`, declared at Line 52.

At Line 58, the `bufsize` variable is set to the text buffer size, plus one for the null character.

Lines 60 and 61 fill the *data_chunk* structure `ftp`, setting the *buf* (memory location) member to the string `text` and the *size* member to `bufsize`. It's important that this memory buffer structure be used for the FTP upload process as it's what the easy curl interface expects.

05-02_ftpmemory.c (Lines 63 to 81)

```
63      /* initialize curl */
64      curl = curl_easy_init();
65
66      puts("Preparing FTP...");
67      /* set options for FPT upload */
68      curl_easy_setopt(curl,
69          CURLOPT_URL, ftp_upload);
70      curl_easy_setopt(curl,
71          CURLOPT_FOLLOWLOCATION, 1L);
72      curl_easy_setopt(curl,
73          CURLOPT_USERPWD, user_pass);
74      curl_easy_setopt(curl,
75          CURLOPT_UPLOAD, 1L);
```

```
76      curl_easy_setopt(curl,
77          CURLOPT_READFUNCTION, read_callback);
78      curl_easy_setopt(curl,
79          CURLOPT_READDATA, &ftp.buf);
80      curl_easy_setopt(curl,
81          CURLOPT_INFILESIZE, ftp.size);
```

Options are set from Line 68 on:

Line 68 sets the URL. Remember the string set at Line 50 is a placeholder.

Line 71 directs curl to obey any URL forwarding.

Line 73 sets the username and password for the FTP upload. These strings could also be placed into the URL string.

Line 74 sets the upload option.

Line 77 specifies the read callback function, which spoon-feeds data to libcurl for the upload.

Line 78 specifies the buffer to upload, which must be part of a memory buffer structure.

Line 80 sets the buffer's size.

05-02_ftpmemory.c (Lines 83 to 99)

```
83      /* request-send upload */
84      res = curl_easy_perform(curl);
85      if( res!=CURLE_OK )
86      {
87          fprintf(stderr,
88              "curl FTP upload fail: %s\n",
89              curl_easy_strerror(res));
99          exit(1);
91      }
92
93      /* cleanup */
94      curl_easy_cleanup(curl);
95      /* inform the user */
96      puts("FTP upload complete");
97
98      return(0);
99  }
```

Finally, the *curl_easy_perform()* function is called. Upon success, the memory buffer, string `text`, is uploaded to the destination FTP site.

Here's a sample run:

```
Preparing FTP...
FTP upload complete
```

The output is boring, but the user enjoys feedback, especially when it proclaims that the upload worked.

If you have any problems, check the URL to confirm that the username and password are correct. If an issue arises, the *curl_easy_strerror()* function at Line 89 should output a descriptive error to assist you.

An important issue to monitor is buffer overflow. If you're creating your own buffer, ensure that its data doesn't extend beyond the buffer's size and stomp over other values in memory. If you build a string to upload, ensure it's capped with a null character.

UPLOAD A FILE DIRECTLY

It took me a while, but eventually I noticed an interesting and useful coincidence. The libcurl callback function is amazingly similar to the *fread()* function.

Here is the *fread()* function's *man* page format:

```
size_t fread(
  void *ptr,
  size_t size,
  size_t nmemb,
  FILE *stream);
```

Here is the prototype for the read callback function:

```
static size_t read_callback(
  void *ptr,
  size_t size,
  size_t nmemb,
  void *user_data);
```

The arguments for both are similar: A storage buffer, `ptr`, two *size_t* arguments, `size` and `nmemb`, and a pointer, `stream` or `user_data`. Both functions return a *size_t* value.

This coincidence gets noticed when you use libcurl to FTP upload a file. Taking advantage of the similarity in arguments makes writing the callback function a snap:

```
static size_t read_callback(
  void *ptr,
```

```
 size_t size,
 size_t nmemb,
 void *user_data)
{
 FILE *local_fp;
 size_t r;

 /* initialize local pointer */
 local_fp = (FILE *)user_data;

 /* read a chunk from the file */
 r = fread(ptr, size, nmemb, local_fp);

 return(r);
}
```

This modified read callback function contains only one
function, *fread()*. This function effectively echoes the same
arguments used for the read callback function itself. Such a
configuration is deal for an FTP file upload, as shown in the
following code, which is split into chunks for easy reference.

05-03_ftpfile1.c (Lines 1 to 22)

```
1   #include <stdio.h>
2   #include <stdlib.h>
3   #include <sys/stat.h>
4   #include <curl/curl.h>
5
6   static size_t read_callback(
7       void *ptr,
8       size_t size,
9       size_t nmemb,
10      void *user_data)
11  {
12      FILE *local_fp;
13      size_t r;
14
15      /* initialize local pointer */
16      local_fp = (FILE *)user_data;
17
18      /* read a chunk from the file */
19      r = fread(ptr, size, nmemb, local_fp);
20
21      return(r);
22  }
```

In this code, the *read_callback()* function reads from an open
file and processes its data, while the *main()* function serves to
open the file, gather file data, and initialize the easy curl
interface.

The *read_callback()* function at Line 6 creates a local copy of the file pointer at Line 16.

At Line 19, the *fread()* function does all the heavy lifting, copying the *read_callback()* function's four arguments exactly. The *fread()* function's return value, *r*, is passed along to return from the *read_callback()* function.

05-03_ftpfile1.c (Lines 24 to 47)

```
24   int main()
25   {
26       char ftp_upload[] = "ftp://127.0.0.0/image1.jpg";
27       char user_pass[] = "username:password";
28       char upload_filename[] = "image1.jpg";
29       CURL *curl;
30       CURLcode res;
31       FILE *input;
32       struct stat finfo;
33       int file_size;
34
35       /* get the file size */
36       stat(upload_filename, &finfo);
37       file_size = finfo.st_size;
38
39       /* open the file */
40       input = fopen( upload_filename, "rb");
41       if( input==NULL)
42       {
43           fprintf(stderr,
44               "Unable to read from %s\n",
45               upload_filename);
46           exit(1);
47       }
```

In the *main()* function, Line 36 calls the *stat()* function to gather details about the file to upload. The file's size is returned from the *finfo* structure's *st_size* member. This value is used function to set the upload size option (Later in Lines 62 to 64).

The return value from the *stat()* function is ignored. The function fails when the file doesn't exist, but this condition is also caught at Line 41, after the file is opened.

05-03_ftpfile1.c (Lines 49 to 69)

```
49       /* initialize curl */
50       curl = curl_easy_init();
51
52       puts("Preparing FTP...");
```

75

```
53    /* set options for FPT upload */
54    curl_easy_setopt(curl,
55        CURLOPT_URL, ftp_upload);
56    curl_easy_setopt(curl,
57        CURLOPT_FOLLOWLOCATION, 1L);
58    curl_easy_setopt(curl,
59        CURLOPT_USERPWD, user_pass);
60    curl_easy_setopt(curl,
61        CURLOPT_UPLOAD, 1L);
62    curl_easy_setopt(curl,
63        CURLOPT_INFILESIZE_LARGE,
64        (curl_off_t)file_size);
65    curl_easy_setopt(curl,
66        CURLOPT_READFUNCTION,
67        read_callback);
68    curl_easy_setopt(curl,
69        CURLOPT_READDATA, input);
```

The options set starting at Line 54 are similar to setting options for uploading a memory chunk, covered in the preceding section.

Line 60 informs libcurl that the operation will be a file upload.

Line 62 sets the CURLOPT_INFILESIZE_LARGE option, specifying the file's size as a *curl_off_t* variable type.

Line 68 uses the CURLOPT_READDATA option to specify the file handle, input. Normally this option would set the memory buffer structure, but here the file handle is passed.

05-03_ftpfile1.c (Lines 71 to 89)

```
71    /* request-send upload */
72    res = curl_easy_perform(curl);
73    if( res!=CURLE_OK )
74    {
75        fprintf(stderr,
76            "curl upload failed: %s\n",
77            curl_easy_strerror(res));
78        fclose(input);
79        exit(1);
80    }
81
82    /* cleanup */
83    curl_easy_cleanup(curl);
84    fclose(input);
85    /* inform the user */
86    puts("FTP upload complete");
87
88    return(0);
89 }
```

The opened file is closed at Line 84, though if the
curl_easy_perform() function fails (at Line 73), the file is closed
at Line 78.

The output from a sample run is boring. Still, the code
uploads the file specified at Line 28 to the address (and
filename) specified at Line 26.

If problems occur, verify the username and password to
ensure that the file exists and has data. And always check for
buffer overflow.

UPLOAD A FILE STORED IN MEMORY

This final example of a file upload becomes very involved: A
file is read, stored in memory, then the memory block is
uploaded. This approach combines methods from the
preceding two sections into one very long source code file,
which I've broken up into sections for easy digestion:

05-04_ftpfile2.c (Lines 1 to 11)

```
1   #include <stdio.h>
2   #include <stdlib.h>
3   #include <string.h>
4   #include <curl/curl.h>
5
6   #define BUFFER_SIZE 2048
7
8   struct data_chunk {
9       char *buf;
10      size_t size;
11  };
```

The 2K defined constant BUFFER_SIZE set at Line 6 is used
when reading the file into memory. The *data_chunk* structure
is defined externally as it's referenced in both the read
callback function as well as in the *main()* function.

05-04_ftpfile2.c (Lines 13 to 39)

```
13  static size_t read_callback(
14      void *ptr,
15      size_t size,
16      size_t nmemb,
17      void *user_data)
18  {
19      struct data_chunk *upload;
20      size_t max;
```

```
21
22      upload = (struct data_chunk *)user_data;
23      max = size*nmemb;
24      if(max<1)
25          return(0);
26
27      if(upload->size)
28      {
29          if(max > upload->size)
30              max = upload->size;
31          memcpy(ptr, upload->buf,max);
32          upload->buf += max;
33          upload->size -= max;
34
35          return(max);
36      }
37
38      return(0);
39 }
```

The read callback function is standard: The passed data
chunk, upload in the function, represents the memory buffer
structure. It's copied into the ptr buffer, at Line 31. From
there it's uploaded during the *curl_easy_perform()* function
call.

05-04_ftpfile2.c (Lines 41 to 72)

```
41 int main()
42 {
43      char address[] = "ftp://127.0.0.0/test.txt";
44      char user_pass[] = "username:password";
45      char filename[] = "test.txt";
46      char in[BUFFER_SIZE];
47      CURL *curl;
48      CURLcode r;
49      struct data_chunk ftp;
50      FILE *fp;
51      int c;
52
53      /* read file */
54      fp = fopen( filename, "r");
55      if( fp==NULL)
56      {
57          fprintf(stderr,
58              "Unable to read %s\n",
59              filename);
60          exit(1);
61      }
62
63      /* initialize buffer */
64      ftp.buf = malloc(1);
65      ftp.size = 0;
```

```
66    if( ftp.buf==NULL )
67    {
68        fprintf(stderr, "Can't init buffer\n");
69        /* close the file */
70        fclose(fp);
71        exit(1);
72    }
```

The *main()* function sets the URL in variable `address` (placeholder set at Line 43), the username and password (Line 44), and filename to upload (line 45), which matches the name at the end of the address.

Line 53 opens the input file for reading into memory. File pointer variable `fp` is used.

Line 64 creates the initial buffer for the memory buffer structure `ftp`, allocating one byte of storage (Line 64) and setting the buffer size to zero (Line 65).

05-04_ftpfile2.c (Lines 74 to 100)

```
74    /* read data from the file
75        into the buffer */
76    while(1)
77    {
78        c=fread(in,sizeof(char),BUFFER_SIZE,fp);
79        ftp.buf=realloc( ftp.buf, ftp.size+c+1);
80        if( ftp.buf==NULL )
81        {
82            fprintf(stderr,"Mem resize error\n");
83            exit(1);
84        }
85        memcpy( &ftp.buf[ftp.size], in, c );
86        ftp.size += c;
87        ftp.buf[ftp.size] = 0;
88        if( c < BUFFER_SIZE)
89        {
90            if( feof(fp) )
91                break;
92            else
93            {
94                fprintf(stderr,"File read error\n");
95                fclose(fp);
96                exit(1);
97            }
98        }
99    }
100   fclose(fp);
```

The *while* loop at line 76 moves data from the open file into memory based on the bytes read at Line 78.

At Line 85, the *memcpy()* function moves the bytes read from the buffer into the memory buffer structure's storage, adjusting the *size* member to reflect the updated value.

Tests are performed starting at Line 88 to determine when the last byte is read: Line 90 confirms, otherwise an error condition is handled.

Line 100 closes the file. At this point in the code, the file's contents are stored in memory, referenced by the memory buffer structure `ftp`.

05-04_ftpfile2.c (Lines 102 to 121)

```
102    /* initialize curl */
103    curl = curl_easy_init();
104
105    printf("Preparing FTP...");
106    /* set options for FPT upload */
107    curl_easy_setopt(curl,
108        CURLOPT_URL, address);
109    curl_easy_setopt(curl,
100        CURLOPT_FOLLOWLOCATION, 1L);
111    curl_easy_setopt(curl,
112        CURLOPT_USERPWD, user_pass);
113    curl_easy_setopt(curl,
114        CURLOPT_UPLOAD, 1L);
115    curl_easy_setopt(curl,
116        CURLOPT_READFUNCTION, read_callback);
117    curl_easy_setopt(curl,
118        CURLOPT_READDATA, &ftp);
119    curl_easy_setopt(curl,
120        CURLOPT_INFILESIZE_LARGE,
121        (curl_off_t)ftp.size);
```

Line 105 outputs a message informing the user that an FTP upload is being prepared.

Line 107 sets the address.

Line 109 activates forwarding for web page redirects.

Line 111 assigns the username and password.

Line 113 directs easy curl to perform an upload.

Lines 115 and 117 identify the read callback function and memory buffer structure, respectively.

Line 119 informs easy curl of the upload file's size.

05-04_ftpfile2.c (Lines 123 to 138)

```
123    /* request-send upload */
124    r = curl_easy_perform(curl);
125    if( r!=CURLE_OK )
126    {
127        fprintf(stderr,"curl upload failed: %s\n",
128            curl_easy_strerror(r));
129        exit(1);
130    }
131
132    /* cleanup */
133    curl_easy_cleanup(curl);
134    /* inform the user */
135    puts("FTP upload complete");
136
137    return(0);
138 }
```

Finally, *curl_easy_perform()* is called at Line 124 and the file upload is attempted. Upon failure, an error message is output at Line 127, otherwise the message at Line 135 informs the user of the operation's success.

The major difference between this code and the preceding two examples is the *while* loop at Line 76. This loop reads from the file and reallocates the buffer ftp.buf to accommodate all data from the file.

This code represented my first attempt to use the easy curl interface to upload a file. I don't know why I chose such a convoluted method, when the earlier example uses far fewer statements. Still, it's an option you can use for whatever reason.

6. MIME Form Data

Another way to upload data to the Internet is to use MIME, the Multipurpose Internet Mail Extensions standard. This standard helps define data, specifically email attachments, by classifying the data type.

With libcurl, a MIME upload supplies web page form data – fill-in-the-blanks stuff. You can write code that automatically fills in those blanks and sets options for a web page form. Further, if the form allows you to upload a file, you can use libcurl to send the file.

The only caution with supplying MIME data is the captcha. This gizmo verifies human input on a web form and is designed specifically to prevent robots from generating data automatically. When you use libcurl to write MIME upload code, your code *is* the robot.

♦ *MIME processing may not be possible with some releases of the libcurl library. Version 7.58 works and was the version tested for this chapter.*

Filling in the blanks

Figure 6-1 illustrates a sample webpage form. It contains two text fields, Name and Email. It also features a Submit button.

Test Form Submission

Name:

Email:

Submit

Figure 6-1: A typical web form.

The form you see is only part of the picture. Other parts include the HTML that codes the form, which includes the internal field names, as well as the code or separate web page that processes the form.

GATHER THE DETAILS

For a MIME data upload, you must know a bit about the webpage form you're trying to fill. Here are the tidbits:

- The name of each field
- The name of the page that processes the form
- The data to send, filling in the fields

Keep in mind that the names you see, such as *Name* and *Email*, shown in Figure 6-1, may not be the same names as the fields within the web page form. (In my example they are, but not always.)

Unless you wrote the web page form yourself, you must do a bit of snooping to discover the details.

Most web browsers let you peek at the raw HTML data used to format a web page. For my example, the following is the relevant HTML from the web page used to create Figure 6-1:

```
<form name="order" action="formsub.php" method="post">
 <p>Name: <input type="text" name="name" size="32"></p>
 <p>Email: <input type="text" name="email" size="32"></p>
 <p><input type="submit" /></p>
</form>
```

The field names are found in the *name* argument for the input tag:

```
<p>Name: <input type="text" name="name" size="32"></p>
```

And:

```
<p>Email: <input type="text" name="email" size="32"></p>
```

The name tags show the fields are named `name` and `email`. The form's "action" is found in the opening *form* tag:

```
<form name="order" action="formsub.php" method="post">
```

The target web page is `formsub.php`. This page receives input supplied by the form. It's the URL to which you send the MIME data.

In your code, you must set the contents of the `name` and `email` fields and send the data to the `formsub.php` webpage for processing.

♦ *If the form is submitted via GET request, you can also look at the final URL (in the address bar) to cull the web page name, field names, and contents. It's that URL, complete with the field names, ampersands, and whatnot, that curl emulates.*

CREATE THE MIME FORM

To supply form data to a webpage, you must create a *curl_mime* variable. This variable acts as a handle to which you add elements available in the form. Each element has a name and value part. The overall process works like this:

1. Create a *curl_mime* handle to reference the form's data.
2. Create a *curl_mimepart* pointer/handle to reference an element in the form.
3. Add the element's name to the *curl_mimepart* handle.
4. Add the element's data to the *curl_mimepart* handle.
5. Repeat Steps 2 through 4 to add more elements.
6. Set the `CURLOPT_MIMEPOST` option to add the *curl_mime* handle to the easy curl request.
7. When the easy curl operation is complete, after calling *curl_easy_cleanup()*, call the *curl_mime_free()* function to free the mime handle and cleanup operations.

The following sections cover the details of these seven steps.

Create the *curl_mime* handle

The entire operation starts with creating a *curl_mime* variable, which works like a handle to reference form data. To retrieve this variable, the *curl_mime_init()* function is used:

```
curl_mime *curl_mime_init(CURL *);
```

The *curl_mime_init()* function's sole argument is the *CURL* handle returned by the *curl_easy_init()* function. The value returned is a *curl_mime* pointer, used with other MIME-related functions to specify the form's fields and supply the data.

Create a *curl_mimepart* variable for each form element

Each field, or form element, is represented by a *curl_mimepart* variable. This pointer variable references a field or form element's name and data. The *curl_mime_addpart()* function creates and returns a *curl_mimepart* variable:

```
curl_mimepart *curl_mime_addpart(curl_mime *);
```

The function's argument is the *curl_mime* pointer from the *curl_mime_init()* function. The value returned is a *curl_mimepart* pointer, which is used in two functions to supply the element name and its value.

Add the element's name

The *curl_mime_name()* function sets the field name:

```
curl_mime_name( mimepart, "Element");
```

The first argument is the *mimepart* pointer. The second is a string representing the element name.

Add the element's data

The *curl_mime_data()* function sets the field's value:

```
CURLcode curl_mime_data(
  curl_mimepart * part,
  const char * data,
  size_t datasize
);
```

The first argument is the *mimepart* pointer. The second is the contents of the element, the data. The third argument is the size of the data, a *size_t* value representing the number of bytes. For strings, the constant can be used.

Here's a sample function:

```
curl_mime_data(mimepart,"Contents", CURL_ZERO_TERMINATED);
```

Above, the data (field contents) for the `mimepart` variable is set to the string "`Contents`". The string is null-character terminated, as set by the third argument.

♦ *The* curl_mime_data() *and* curl_mime_name() *functions can appear in either order.*

86

Create additional fields

To add additional fields, use the *curl_mime_addpart()* function to create another *curl_mimepart* pointer for the next field.

♦ *You need not supply data for every field in the form. If the fields are required, submit them. Otherwise, only submit what's necessary.*

Set the *CURLOPT_MIMEPOST* option

To inform easy curl of the form data, call the *curl_easy_setopt()* function with the CURLOPT_MIMEPOST constant as the second argument, as the *curl_mime* pointer as the third:

```
curl_easy_setopt( curl, CURLOPT_MIMEPOST, form);
```

Above, form is the *curl_mime* variable returned from the *curl_mime_init()* function, and used with the *curl_mime_addpart()* function.

Clean-up

After completing the easy curl operation, call the *curl_mime_free()* function with the *curl_mime* pointer variable as its argument:

```
curl_mime_free(form);
```

The process of creating form data is involved, but it follows a logical sequence. Your code creates pieces – pointer variables – for each step of the process: one for the form itself, another for each field or element in the form, then a pair of items for the field name and its data.

SAMPLE CODE

The following code submits form data based on the fields presented in Figure 6-1, name and email. The web page reference, formsub.php, is bogus, so the code compiles but doesn't work unless you have a web server installed on your computer and the given page happens to exist and properly process the form data.

06-01_mimeform.c (Lines 1 to 15)

```
1 | #include <stdio.h>
```

```
 2    #include <stdlib.h>
 3    #include <curl/curl.h>
 4
 5    int main()
 6    {
 7        char address[] = "http://127.0.0.0/formsub.php";
 8        CURL *curl;
 9        CURLcode res;
10        curl_mime *form = NULL;
11        curl_mimepart *name_field = NULL;
12        curl_mimepart *email_field = NULL;
13
14        /* initialize curl */
15        curl = curl_easy_init();
```

Variables are declared and easy curl is initialized at the start of the *main()* function.

The *curl_mimepart* pointers `name_field` and `email_field` are initialized to NULL to avoid compiler warnings.

06-01_mimeform.c (Lines 1 to 15)

```
17        /* create the form */
18        form = curl_mime_init(curl);
19            /* add the name field */
20        name_field = curl_mime_addpart(form);
21        curl_mime_name( name_field, "name");
22        curl_mime_data( name_field, "George Washington",
23            CURL_ZERO_TERMINATED);
24            /* add the email field */
25        email_field = curl_mime_addpart(form);
26        curl_mime_name( email_field, "email");
27        curl_mime_data( email_field, "gw@potus.gov",
28            CURL_ZERO_TERMINATED);
```

At Line 18, the *curl_mime_init()* function is called, its value returned in the `form` variable.

The `name_field` variable is created at Line 20, added to the `form` variable. Its name and data portions added at Lines 21 and 22.

The `email_field` variable is created at line 20, also added to the `form` variable.

The effect of these statements is to build the form's data.

06-01_mimeform.c (Lines 1 to 15)

```
30        /* set curl options */
31        curl_easy_setopt(curl, CURLOPT_MIMEPOST,form );
```

```
32        curl_easy_setopt(curl, CURLOPT_URL,address );
33
34        /* send the form to the page */
35        res = curl_easy_perform(curl);
36        if( res!=CURLE_OK )
37        {
38            fprintf(stderr, "Unable to upload form\n");
39            exit(1);
40        }
41
42        /* cleanup */
43        curl_easy_cleanup(curl);
44            /* and release the form */
45        curl_mime_free(form);
46
47        return(0);
48    }
```

The easy curl interface is made aware of the form and its data at Line 31. Line 32 sets the URL. That's it for a form upload: *curl_easy_perform()* is called at Line 35.

Line 43 cleans up the easy curl interface. Line 45 frees the form pointer.

Here's sample output:

```
<!doctype html>
<html>
<head>
<meta charset="UTF-8">
<title>Form Submitted</title>
</head>
<body>
<h1>Form Submitted</h1><p>You are 'George Washington'
with email 'gw@potus.gov'</p></body>
</html>
```

Figure 6-2 shows how this HTML text looks when displayed in a web browser.

Form Submitted

You are 'George Washington' with email 'gw@potus.gov'

Figure 6-2. The form data was uploaded via a libcurl program.

ELEMENT OPTIONS

Not every element in a form is a text input field. Some, such as checkboxes and radio buttons, require special types of data if you're to generate form input in your code.

Checkbox

For a checkbox, the data field is the string "on" for a checked box.

Radio button

For a radio button, the field name is the button's name with the data field as the value. For example, for these buttons:

```
<input type="radio" name="station" value="95.5">
<input type="radio" name="station" value="96.9">
<input type="radio" name="station" value="98.1">
<input type="radio" name="station" value="99.5">
```

The name field would be "station" above. The data field would be one of the values, whichever one you wanted to select.

Selection list

For a selection list, the field name is the list's name and the data field is the name of the selection. For example:

```
<select name="country">
```

The field name is country. The data is one of the options presented:

```
<option>France</option>
<option>Germany</option>
<option>Italy</option>
<option>Poland</option>
```

The string set between option tags is the string supplied for the *curl_mime_name()* function. For example, Germany would be the data to supply for the country field.

The only unique item to specify is a file upload, which is covered in the next section.

90

Uploading a file as MIME data

It's possible to upload a file by using a web page form. The form has a gizmo that lets you browse for and select the file. Click the Submit or similar button and the file is sent off to the Internet.

You can use the libcurl library to send a file to a web page just as if it were submitted by using a web page form. The process combines the techniques of specifying MIME data as well as FTP upload.

THE UPLOAD FORM

Figure 6-3 illustrates a crude web page form for uploading a file. The Choose File button is clicked to summon an Open dialog box, which you use to browse for and select a file.

Test Form Submission

Choose File   No file chosen

Submit

Figure 6-3: A crude file upload form.

The HTML `input` tag is used to create the Choose File button. The `type` option is set to `file` and the `name` option references the local filename submitted:

```
<input name="filename" type="file" />
```

The form's target, set by the *action* option in the *form* tag, swallows the file by using whatever magic it can muster. For most web file uploads, PHP code is used to move the file from temporary storage to a permanent location or to further process the file.

When you use *curl* to emulate the form, the file specified is uploaded to the target web page, supplied just as if it were selected by using the Choose File button and submitted as form data.

EASY CURL FORM DATA OPTIONS

To upload a file in your C code, you must combine the techniques for a MIME form upload with an FTP file transfer – but not all the FTP file transfer code. The steps work like this:

1. **Open the file for reading.**
2. **Create a libcurl MIME form and add a field with the proper field name and the filename to upload as the data.**
3. **Specify a read callback function to handle reading the file's data.**
4. **Clean-up curl, free the form, and close the file.**

Unlike some FTP file upload methods, you need not fill a memory buffer structure to upload the file; just open it. The following sections provide details for each of the steps:

Open the file for reading

Open the file as you would any file. I recommend using the "rb" argument to the *fopen()* function to read the file in binary mode:

```
fp = fopen( file, "rb");
```

Create a libcurl MIME form

Use the *curl_mime_init()* and *curl_mime_addpart()* functions as described earlier in this chapter:

```
form = curl_mime_init(curl);
field = curl_mime_addpart(form);
```

To specify the field, or element, describing the file, first use the *curl_mime_name()* function to set the same name as the upload name in the form. For example, if the upload HTML code is:

```
<input name="file" type="file" />
```

The *curl_mime_name()* statement is:

```
curl_mime_name( field, "file");
```

Instead of using the *curl_mime_data()* function to specify the file, use the *curl_mime_filedata()* function:

```
curl_mime_filedata(field,file);
```

Its two arguments are the *curl_mimepart* variable returned from the *curl_mime_addpart()* function, `field` above, and the name of the file uploaded, string `file` above.

♦ *You do not specify the file handle with the* curl_mime_filedata() *function.*

Set the read callback function

As with an FTP upload, two options are set to specify the uploaded file by using the *curl_easy_setopt()* function:

First, CURLOPT_READFUNCTION, with the callback function's name as the third argument:

```
curl_easy_setopt(curl, CURLOPT_READFUNCTION,
  read_callback);
```

Second, CURLOPT_READDATA, with the open *FILE* pointer as its third argument:

```
curl_easy_setopt(curl, CURLOPT_READDATA,fp);
```

The callback function used is identical to the one shown for an FPT upload: Effectively, you pass along all the read callback function's arguments to the *fread()* function for processing.

SAMPLE CODE

The following code demonstrates how to fill in form data based on the sample form illustrated earlier in Figure 6-3. The website listed in the code (Line 23) is bogus; it should be replaced with a legitimate action page to digest the form data. The filename is supplied for demonstration only.

I've broken up the listing into sections relevant to the program's duties.

93

06-02_formupload.c (Lines 1 to 19)

```
1    #include <stdio.h>
2    #include <stdlib.h>
3    #include <sys/stat.h>
4    #include <curl/curl.h>
5
6    static size_t read_callback(
7        void *ptr,
8        size_t size,
9        size_t nmemb,
10       void *userdata)
11   {
12       FILE *local;
13       size_t r;
14
15       local = (FILE *)userdata;
16       r = fread(ptr,size,nmemb,local);
17
18       return(r);
19   }
```

In the code you find the simple version of the *read_callback()* function, starting at Line 6. It effectively passes through the arguments to the *fread()* function at Line 16, which is what processes the input file for upload.

06-02_formupload.c (Lines 21 to 37)

```
21   int main()
22   {
23       char address[] = "https://127.0.0.0/formsub.php";
24       char file[] = "report.pdf";
25       CURL *curl;
26       CURLcode res;
27       curl_mime *form = NULL;
28       curl_mimepart *field = NULL;
29       FILE *fp;
30
31       /* open the file */
32       fp = fopen( file, "rb");
33       if( fp==NULL )
34       {
35           fprintf(stderr, "Unable to open %s\n", file);
36           exit(1);
37       }
```

In the *main()* function, variables are declared. Remember that the URL `address` at Line 23 is bogus. The filename `file` at Line 24 is also a placeholder.

06-02_formupload.c (Lines 39 and 40)

```
39    /* initialize curl */
40    curl = curl_easy_init();
```

Curl is initialized at Line 40. The next step is to build the form.

06-02_formupload.c (Lines 42 to 47)

```
42    /* create the form */
43    form = curl_mime_init(curl);
44        /* add the file field */
45    field = curl_mime_addpart(form);
46    curl_mime_name(field,"file");
47    curl_mime_filedata(field,file);
```

Line 43 creates the *curl_mime* variable form. This variable is used at Line 45 to add an element, saved in *curl_mimepart* variable field.

At Line 46, the *curl_mime_name()* function sets the field name, file.

At line 47, the curl_*mime_filedata()* function assigns the filename string file to the field variable. Note that this option isn't the file handle; it's the filename.

The form is filled.

06-02_formupload.c (Lines 49 to 54)

```
49    /* set curl options */
50    curl_easy_setopt(curl, CURLOPT_MIMEPOST,form);
51    curl_easy_setopt(curl, CURLOPT_READFUNCTION,
52        read_callback);
53    curl_easy_setopt(curl, CURLOPT_READDATA,fp);
54    curl_easy_setopt(curl, CURLOPT_URL,address);
```

Easy curl options are set starting at Line 50. The first is to add the completed form to the *CURL* handle curl.

Line 51 identifies the read callback function.

Line 53 specifies the open file handle, fp. This argument would otherwise be a memory buffer structure.

Line 54 sets the upload address, the web page that digests the form and does whatever magic needs to be done with the file.

06-02_formupload.c (Lines 56 to 73)

```
56      /* send the form to the page */
57      res = curl_easy_perform(curl);
58      if( res!=CURLE_OK )
59      {
60          fprintf(stderr, "failed: %s\n",
61              curl_easy_strerror(res));
62          exit(1);
63      }
64
65      /* cleanup */
66      curl_easy_cleanup(curl);
67          /* release the form */
68      curl_mime_free(form);
69          /* and close the file */
70      fclose(fp);
71
72      return(0);
73  }
```

The easy curl call is made at Line 57. Errors are handled starting at Line 58.

For the cleanup: Line 66 closes-up easy curl, Line 68 frees the MIME form data, and Line 70 closes the open file.

The sample run shows whatever output is generated by the action page. So, what happens with the output depends on what the page does.

If the uploaded file somehow becomes viewable on the website, you can access it after the program runs. For example, if uploading an image file, you can browse to the image's location to view it.

7. Fancy Curl Tricks

The libcurl library is quite extensive, offering a potpourri of interesting options and features, from the necessary to the obscure.

The good news is that the library's online documentation is extensive and sample files are readily available. Better news is that I've pulled a few of the more useful features and plopped them into this chapter for your education and enjoyment.

Going verbose

Like any programmer, my code occasionally doesn't fly straight the first time it's compiled. What follows is a stream of expletives, irrational rage, and a bitter taste of futility. A better approach is to resolve the problem through troubleshooting.

To make libcurl troubleshooting easier, activate its verbose option. It may not help with typical C code issues, but for diagnosing libcurl and connection issues, it's nifty.

Activate verbose output by using the CURLOPT_VERBOSE option with the *curl_easy_setopt()* function. The third argument is 1L:

```
curl_easy_setopt( curl, CURLOPT_VERBOSE, 1L);
```

Here's some sample code:

07-01_verbose.c

```
1  #include <stdio.h>
2  #include <stdlib.h>
3  #include <curl/curl.h>
4
5  int main()
6  {
7      CURL *curl;
8      char url[] =
9          "https://c-for-dummies.com/curl_test.txt";
10
11     /* initialize easy curl */
12     curl = curl_easy_init();
```

```
13    if(curl)
14    {
15        curl_easy_setopt(curl,
16            CURLOPT_VERBOSE, 1L);
17        curl_easy_setopt(curl,
18            CURLOPT_URL, url);
19        curl_easy_perform(curl);
20        curl_easy_cleanup(curl);
21    }
22
23    return(0);
24 }
```

The code is extremely brief, fetching the page referenced at Lines 8 and 9 and sending text to standard output. Because the CURLOPT_VERBOSE setting is activated at Lines 15 and 16, however, the output is extensive and overwhelming.

The first part of the output (sent to the standard error device, not standard output) lists connection information, then details about the server. If HTTPS protocol is used, particulars of the certificates appear. Server information is also presented.

The final part of output is the web page contents, which are sent to standard output.

♦ *Because the verbose items are output to the standard error device, you can't capture them by redirecting output.*

Processing multiple files

The command prompt version of *curl* offers options for regular expressions. You can specify these options to fetch multiple files. For example:

```
curl http://site.com/images/pic[00-99].png
```

The above command fetches 100 files from `site.com` (a bogus website), from `pic00.png` through `pic99.png`. Similar settings are used to fetch files from multiple pages, as provided in the *curl man* page or online documentation.

This multiple file method has no corresponding option in libcurl. If your goal is to fetch multiple web pages or files, you make multiple *curl_easy_perform()* calls, each with the address or webpage specified directly.

If you use the `--libcurl` option at the command prompt, this approach is confirmed by examining the corresponding libcurl code: Multiple calls are made to *curl_easy_perform()*, each with its own set of options specifying whatever to fetch.

Alas, there is no secret.

Eating cookies

Libcurl features a handful of web page cookie options, which allow you to supply cookie information for a website. As with the MIME upload option, it's necessary to know about a website's cookies and their contents before you randomly upload cookie data.

COOKIE RECIPE

Cookies, also called magic cookies, were invented by Netscape to retain information between web page visits. The intent was that tidbits of info could be recalled, for example, so you would be recognized as a return visitor.

The web page initializes a cookie as a string of text. It contains a name, content, and an expiration value. This information is stored on the client's computer. It's supplied automatically, returned to the website on the next visit.

The web page server sets and retrieves cookies as part of the HTTP header. The `Set-Cookie` directive creates the cookie.

A session cookie, which expires when the user browses away from the site, consists of a name and value pair, as in:

```
Set-Cookie: sound=on
```

This session cookie is named `sound` and its value is `on`. This data is stored temporarily.

A persistent cookie features a timeout or expiration date:

```
Set-Cookie: user=dang; Expires=Sun, 01 Jan 2023 00:00:00
GMT
```

The cookie's name is `user`, value `dang`, and its expiration date is listed above. When the user re-visits the site, the browser returns the cookie, `user=dang`. The information is supplied in the page request as line of text, such as:

`Cookie: user=dang`

Likewise, libcurl sends the cookie data as part of the HTTP header, providing it to the web page for whatever purposes required.

WEBSITE COOKIES

Unless you designed the website where you desire to send a cookie, it's not obvious which cookies are in use and what their purpose could be. Most web browsers let you examine the cookies used by a site, though the method differs between them.

In Google's Chrome, click on the icon found on the far left of the address bar. Choose Cookies from the menu as shown in Figure 7-1.

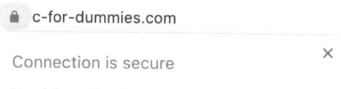

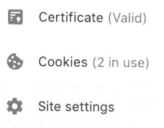

Figure 7-1: Displaying cookies in Google Chrome.

The Cookies In Use window shows a list of site and other cookies (advertising). Choose one to view the Name and Content values. Timeout information is also shown.

Of course, the cookie values mean nothing absent any context. In fact, most cookies are complex, consisting of hexadecimal values that are relevant only to the site itself.

LIBCURL COOKIES

A single option set by the *curl_easy_setopt()* function supplies a cookie string for a website. The option is the function's second argument, CURLOPT_COOKIE. The third argument is the cookie string. For example:

```
curl_easy_setopt( curl, CURLOPT_COOKIE, "name=dang");
```

Multiple cookies can be passed by separating each with a semicolon:

```
"name=dang; status=alive"
```

The following code sends a cookie to the address specified. The details are provided for illustrative purposes only as the site is bogus and the cookie data is arbitrary, yet the code outlines the libcurl cookie-setting procedure.

07-02_cookie.c

```
1   #include <stdio.h>
2   #include <stdlib.h>
3   #include <curl/curl.h>
4
5   int main()
6   {
7       char address[] = "http://127.0.0.0/";
8       char cookie[] = "username=dang";
9       CURL *curl;
10      CURLcode r;
11
12      curl = curl_easy_init();
13      if( curl==NULL )
14      {
15          fprintf(stderr,"Unable to curl\n");
16          exit(1);
17      }
18
19      curl_easy_setopt(curl,CURLOPT_URL,address);
20      curl_easy_setopt(curl,CURLOPT_COOKIE,cookie);
21
```

```
22        r = curl_easy_perform(curl);
23        if( r!=CURLE_OK)
24        {
25            fprintf(stderr,"Curl error: %s\n",
26                curl_easy_strerror(r));
27            exit(1);
28        }
29
30        curl_easy_cleanup(curl);
31        puts("Cookies sent");
32        return(0);
33    }
```

The website at Line 7 is bogus. To test the code, I used a real webpage that would respond to the cookie specified at Line 8. The cookie name is username and the data is dang.

Line 20 sets the cookie data.

The remainder of the code is standard, initializing easy curl and then closing it up. A message it output to the user confirming that the operation succeeded.

Here is sample output, assuming a web page is designed to consume the cookie submitted:

```
<!doctype html>
<html>
<head>
<title>Test</title>
</head>
<body>
<p>Cookie received: 'dang'</p>
</body>
</html>Cookies sent
```

The web page shows a single line of text, displaying the value of the username cookie:

```
Cookie received: 'dang'
```

The last part of output, Cookies sent, is generated by the libcurl program.

Generating email

Another URL the libcurl library lets you access is SMTP, the Simple Mail Transfer Protocol. It's the protocol designed to deliver mail on the Internet. By using libcurl, you can code a C program that uses an SMTP server to send mail.

♦ *SMTP is different from the POP (Post Office Protocol) used to collect email and IMAP (Internet Mail Access Protocol) used for webmail and other mail services.*

VARIOUS SMTP PIECES

The process involved with sending SMTP mail is complex and subtly different from other protocols used in libcurl. To use libcurl with the SMTP protocol, the following pieces must be assembled:

- The message string
- An *upload_status* structure
- A payload source function that processes the message contents
- Various options to set the sender, recipient(s), usernames, passwords, and so on

All parts of the message must be assembled properly and supplied according to the SMTP protocol. Further, you must have an account on the SMTP server to process the message.

The following sections cover the details of the four pieces required to use libcurl to send an SMTP email message.

Message string

The message string includes both the header as well as the message contents. It must be formatted in a specific way to ensure that the SMTP server properly digests the entire thing.

Text in the message is stored as a series of strings in a pointer array – and array of strings. Each line ends with a carriage return (\r) and newline (\n) combination. The final line, marking the end of the *char* pointer array, is a NULL string.

The message header includes a timestamp and the To, From, and Subject fields. It might also include other fields as set by the SMTP standard; refer to any online reference for the protocol's specifics.

The message body is separated from the header by an empty or blank line. Here's an example:

```
const char *message[] = {
  "Date: Sat, 16 Oct 2021 14:00:00 +800\r\n",
  "To: joe_user@mail.com\r\n",
  "From: somebody@site.com\r\n",
  "Subject: Test message\r\n",
  "\r\n", /* blank line */
  "Hello! This is a test\r\n",
  (char *)NULL
};
```

This string is best declared globally, external to all functions in the source code file. You can declare it in part of a function, but then things get hinky when passing a pointer array.

If you must build the string on the fly, declare the empty pointer array externally, then allocate and fill it from within a function.

The *upload_status* structure

An *upload_status* structure monitors lines read from the message. It contains one member, an integer:

```
struct up_stat {
  int lines_read;
};
```

This structure must be declared eternally as it's used by both the payload source function and the *main()* function.

The payload source function

Similar to the read callback and write callback functions for file transfer, the payload source function is what spoon-feeds the message contents line-by-line for uploading. This function performs two tasks:

- Ensure that information (a line in the message) is available to upload. If not, the function exits.
- Transfer a line of text from the message buffer (the array of strings) to the buffer used by libcurl for uploading.

Here is a typical payload source function, conveniently named *payload_source()*:

```
static size_t payload_source(void *ptr, size_t size,
size_t nmemb, void *userp)
{
  struct up_stat *upcount;
```

```
const char *data;
size_t len;

upcount = (struct up_stat *)userp;

if( (size==0) || (nmemb==0) || ((size*nmemb)<1))
{
    return(0);
}

data = message[upcount->lines_read];
if( data!=NULL )
{
    len = strlen(data);
    memcpy(ptr, data, len);
    upcount->lines_read++;
    return(len);
}

return(0);
}
```

The function's argument list is similar to the read/write callback function: `ptr` is libcurl's internal buffer; `size` is the size of each item to read; `nmemb` is the number of items or elements; `userp` is the user data passed to the function.

The complex *if* test ensures that data is available to write. If not, the function returns zero, meaning the upload is complete.

When data is available, the *memcpy()* function transfers the user-supplied data – one string from the buffer – to libcurl's internal buffer. The *lines_read* member of the *upload_status* (*up_stat* in the code) structure is updated, and the length of the string read is returned.

Options to set

The easy curl interface must be made aware of all the pieces covered so far in the STMP process, as well as a few others. Here are the constants used with the *curl_easy_setopt()* function to set the necessary options:

CURLOPT_URL sets the SMTP server's address. It uses the URL SMTP:// and you must have an account on the server to use it. (I've not heard of any open or free SMTP servers.)

CURLOPT_USERNAME assigns your account's username.

105

CURLOPT_PASSWORD assigns your account's password.

CURLOPT_MAIL_FROM sets a string representing the email sender. The email address can be enclosed in angle brackets, prefixed by the username. This is the same string that appears in the message text header.

CURLOPT_MAIL_RCPT sets the recipient list, as held in the pointer structure *curl_slist*. This is the same list that appears in the message header.

This *curl_slist* pointer variable is filled by using the *curl_slist_append()* function:

```
struct curl_slist *curl_slist_append(
  struct curl_slist * list,
  const char * string
);
```

The *curl_slist* vaiable is a pointer preset to NULL when it's declared:

```
struct curl_slist *rec = NULL;
```

Above, *curl_slist* pointer rec is is used twice in the *curl_slist_append()* function, both as an argument and as the return value:

```
rec = curl_slist_append(rec,"<joe_user@mail.com>");
```

The *curl_slist_append()* function appends recipient strings to the list and an uninitialized pointer is a Bad Thing. Therefore, the call above is kosher, adding the recipient string (the function's second argument) to the recipient list.

Multiple calls can be made to *curl_slist_append()* to build the list of To and Cc recipients.

After building the recipient list, the *curl_slist* pointer variable is specified in a *curl_easy_setopt()* function call:

```
curl_easy_setopt(curl, CURLOPT_MAIL_RCPT, rec);
```

CURLOPT_READFUNCTION sets the name of the payload source function.

CURLOPT_READDATA specifies the address of the *upload_status* structure variable.

CURLOPT_UPLOAD is set to 1L as it would be for any file upload.

With all the options set, a call is made to *curl_easy_perform()* to process and send the email.

SAMPLE CODE

The following code uses libcurl to sign into an SMTP server and send an email message. The server address, username, password, and email addresses are all placeholders; you must have an account on an SMTP server for the code to work.

I've split the code into chunks to avoid the Great Wall of Code in this book:

07-03_mailsend.c (Lines 1 to 18)

```
1   #include <stdio.h>
2   #include <stdlib.h>
3   #include <string.h>
4   #include <curl/curl.h>
5
6   const char *message[] = {
7       "Date: Sat, 16 Oct 2021 14:00:00 +800\r\n",
8       "To: joe_user@mail.com\r\n",
9       "From: somebody@site.com\r\n",
10      "Subject: Test message\r\n",
11      "\r\n", /* blank line */
12      "Hello! This is a test\r\n",
13      (char *)NULL
14  };
15
16  struct up_stat {
17      int lines_read;
18  };
```

The message at Line 6 is a *const char* pointer array, which translates into English as an array of strings. The strings represent the message one line at a time, each one ending with a carriage return and newline combination, \r\n.

The message content is split into header and message content portions; a blank line (Line 11) separates the two.

The header contains basic information but can also contain other fields common to email messages, including a message ID and other details I'm too lazy to look up. The minimum, shown above, works in this code. (Well, it would work if the server address and other vitals were valid.)

The final string in the message (Line 13) must be NULL, which is how the library determines that the message is complete.

The upload status structure is defined as up_stat in this code. (I abbreviated the name to keep the code's lines short.) The sole member is *lines_read*.

07-03_mailsend.c (Lines 20 to 47)

```
20   static size_t paysrc(
21         void *ptr,
22         size_t size,
23         size_t nmemb,
24         void *userp)
25   {
26         struct up_stat *upcount;
27         const char *data;
28         size_t len;
29
30         upcount = (struct up_stat *)userp;
31
32         if( (size==0) || (nmemb==0) || ((size*nmemb)<1))
33         {
34             return(0);
35         }
36
37         data = message[upcount->lines_read];
38         if( data!=NULL )
39         {
40             len = strlen(data);
41             memcpy(ptr, data, len);
42             upcount->lines_read++;
43             return(len);
44         }
45
46         return(0);
47   }
```

The payload source function, *paysrc()*, starts at Line 20. It has four arguments.

At Line 32, a test is performed to determine whether the entire message has been read. If so, zero is returned at Line 34.

The message's lines are processed at Line 37. The data pointer references the starting point in the message[] array where the next line is to be processed. Line 40 gathers the line's length, then Line 41 copies the line of text into libcurl's internal buffer. The number of lines read is updated and the line's length (len) is returned.

If the data buffer is empty, the *return* statement at Line 46 is executed.

07-03_mailsend.c (Lines 49 to 64)

```
49   int main()
50   {
51       const char address[] = "smtp://127.0.0.0";
52       struct up_stat upcount;
53       struct curl_slist *rec = NULL;
54       CURL *curl;
55       CURLcode r;
56
57       upcount.lines_read = 0;
58
59       curl = curl_easy_init();
60       if( curl==NULL )
61       {
62           fprintf(stderr,"Unable to curl\n");
63           exit(1);
64       }
```

The *main()* function starts by declaring its variables at Line 51 with the SMTP server's address.

The *curl_slist* pointer variable rec is initialized to NULL at Line 53. This step is important as the *curl_slist_append()* function, used later in the code, assumes the pointer to be initialized.

The *upcount* structure's *lines_read* member is initialized to zero at Line 57. This step is also important as the variable is used immediately and without initialization to zero (the start of the message) random garbage might be sent.

The easy curl interface is started at Line 59.

07-03_mailsend.c (Lines 66 to 82)

```
66       curl_easy_setopt(curl,
67           CURLOPT_URL, address);
68       curl_easy_setopt(curl,
69           CURLOPT_USERNAME, "user");
70       curl_easy_setopt(curl,
71           CURLOPT_PASSWORD, "password");
72       curl_easy_setopt(curl,
73           CURLOPT_MAIL_FROM, "<somebody@site.com>");
74       rec=curl_slist_append(rec,"<joe_user@mail.com>");
75       curl_easy_setopt(curl,
76           CURLOPT_MAIL_RCPT, rec);
```

```
77    curl_easy_setopt(curl,
78        CURLOPT_READFUNCTION, paysrc);
79    curl_easy_setopt(curl,
80        CURLOPT_READDATA, &upcount);
81    curl_easy_setopt(curl,
82        CURLOPT_UPLOAD, 1L);
```

The code chunk from Lines 66 through 83 initializes options for the SMTP mail-sending operation. These options are discussed earlier in this chapter.

07-03_mailsend.c (Lines 84 to 95)

```
84    r = curl_easy_perform(curl);
85    if( r!=CURLE_OK )
86    {
87        fprintf(stderr,"Curl failed: %s\n",
88            curl_easy_strerror(r));
89        exit(1);
90    }
91
92    curl_easy_cleanup(curl);
93
94    return(0);
95 }
```

After everything is set, easy curl is performed at Line 84. Errors are handled if necessary, then Line 92 wraps up the curl operation.

The only thing missing from this code is standard output. If successful, the program exits without generating a message. Otherwise, the message is sent and received in whatever inbox you selected. For my test run, I sent mail from my ISP account to Gmail. It appeared instantly.

Index

A

anonymous FTP
    curl command line 19
    libcurl 63
Anonymous FTP
    libcurl 63
APT 26

B

backslash 19
binary data
    fetching with libcurl 53
buffer overflow 73

C

callback function 50, 56, 57
    sample code 58
captcha...................................83
CodeBlocks in Windows 27
CodeBlocks project 27
compiling
    command prompt 30
    linker errors.....................31
cookies 99
curl
    configuration file 15
    definition 13
    fetch web page...............13
    global configuration file ..17
    options, terse verbose.....14
    regular expressions 14
CURL handle 35
curl protocols 20
curl_easy_cleanup() 37
curl_easy_init() 35
    testing for errors 40
curl_easy_perform().............37

curl_easy_setopt().........36, 59
curl_easy_strerror().......37, 47
CURL_ERROR_SIZE 45
curl_mime variable 85
curl_mime_addpart() 86
curl_mime_data() 86
curl_mime_filedata() 93
curl_mime_free() 87
curl_mime_init()...................85
curl_mime_name() 86
curl_mimepart variable........86
curl_slist_append().............106
curl_version() 32
curl_version_info() 33
CURLcode value....................37
CURLE_OK constant 44
CURLOPT_BUFFERSIZE 40
CURLOPT_COOKIE..............101
CURLOPT_ERRORBUFFER.....45
CURLOPT_FOLLOWLOCATION
    ....41, 42
CURLOPT_FORWARDLOCATIO
    N.......................................43
CURLOPT_HTTP_VERSION ...41
CURLOPT_INFILESIZE_LARGE
   76
CURLOPT_MAIL_FROM 106
CURLOPT_MAIL_RCPT........106
CURLOPT_MAXREDIRS ...41, 44
CURLOPT_MIMEPOST 87
CURLOPT_NOPROGRESS 41
CURLOPT_READDATA 76
CURLOPT_TCP_KEEPALIVE ...41
CURLOPT_USERAGENT 41
CURLOPT_USERPWD............67
CURLOPT_VERBOSE 97
CURLOPT_WRITEDATA.........50
CURLOPT_WRITEFUNCTION 50

libcurl FTP.........................64

CURLoption constant 36

D

data_chunk structure...........77
DICT...20

E

easy curl interface 35
error buffer 45
error checking 48

F

fetching a web page
    libcurl 37
file handle 50
form elements......................90
forwarding
    libcurl 42
fread() 73
FTP
    curl command prompt 21
FTP authentication 63
FTP memory upload 69
FTP passwords
    libcurl 66
FTP upload from memory 68

H

Homebrew 26
HTML form checkbox 90
HTML form field names 84
HTML form radio button......90
HTML form selection list 90
HTML GET request 85
HTML input tag 91
HTTP POST
    curl command prompt 21

L

libcurl API 34

libcurl email 102
libcurl header files...............28
libcurl library
    downloading instructions 25
libcurl switch 23
libcurl version number 29
LIBCURL_VERSION string......30
Linux
    in Windows 10.................13

M

memcpy() 59, 80
memory buffer structure56, 69
message string
    for SMTP upload...........103
MIME
    definition 83
MIME file upload.................91
MIME upload 83

P

package manager.................26
payload source function 104
progress bar 41
progress meter.....................16

R

read callback function..........69
    MIME upload...................93
    using fread() 74
realloc() 58

S

save the web page text to a file
    curl command line...........19
Saving a web page to a file...49
session cookie 99
SMTP 103
standard error device..........98

stat()......................................75
Storing web data in memory55
sudo......................................26
Super User account..............26

U

upload files
    curl command prompt 20
upload_status structure.....104
URL encoding 18, 22, 68
user agent 41
username and password
    libcurl option 67
Username and password
    in a URL 66

usernames and passwords
    curl command line...........17

W

web form file upload
    curl command prompt 22
webpage form......................83
webpage forwarding............41
write callback function...52, 61
write function 50

X

Xcode
    building a libcurl program
       31

Also by Dan Gookin

Check out these other titles available from Dan Gookin at the Amazon Kindle store:

Dan Gookin's Guide to Ncurses Programming

Dan Gookin's Guide to XML and JSON Programming

Beginning Programming with C For Dummies

Android Phones and Tablets For Dummies

Word 2019 For Dummies

Word 2016 For Professionals For Dummies

PCs For Dummies

Laptops For Dummies

Visit my website for all current titles:
https://www.wambooli.com/titles/

www.ingramcontent.com/pod-product-compliance
Lightning Source LLC
Chambersburg PA
CBHW031243050326
40690CB00007B/938